BEWARE OF OBSESSION

BEWARE OF OBSESSION

A Mindful Approach to Healing, Regaining Control, and Restoring Peace of Mind

BY

KURT GASSNER

Beware of Obsession
Kurt Gassner

All rights reserved
First Edition, 2022
© Kurt Gassner, 2022

It is unlawful to reproduce, copy, or distribute any portion of this study using electronic methods or otherwise. The reproduction of these materials is disallowed, with the exception of written distributor authorization. All resources are retained.

This statement of principles is approved and endorsed by the American Bar Association Committee and the Publications and Associations Commission.

The statistics herein are solely for instructional purposes, and the details cannot be explicitly guaranteed.

The markings used shall be without permission, and without the approval or the help of the proprietors. All logos and trademarks in this book are for information purposes only and are held explicitly by individuals who are not affiliated with this document.

Impressum
My-mindguide – The publishing trademarke of trendguide Capital GmbH, Klenzestr. 42a, 80469 Munich, Germany.

Reg. Nr. HRB Munich 206639, VAT 152 123 159, CEO: Kurt Friedrich Gassner
Web: www.my-mindguide.com, mail: gassner@my-mindguide.com

Paperback ISBN: 978-3-98793-023-2
Hardback ISBN: 978-3-98793-024-9

Table of Contents

Obssession

My-mindguide.com

WHY I WROTE THIS BOOK AND WHY IT'S IMPORTANT FOR THE READER

The aim of this book is to ensure that readers will be equipped to detect and heal from obsession.

Do you have persistent and intrusive thoughts, mental images, or physical sensations? Have your efforts to avoid or escape this agony failed to provide you with long-term and much-needed relief? *Beware of Obsession* is a ground-breaking book that does what no other title has done before: effortlessly blending mindfulness-based remedies with cutting-edge, exposure-based strategies in a self-help format.

The curse of anxiety has been with us since the dawn of time. It's the price humans pay for being the only animal capable of looking in the mirror and imagining how things *should* be. Under normal conditions, this can lead to tremendous accomplishments, yet the ability to ponder, want, plan, and feel occasionally becomes an affliction.

- Do you ever find yourself fretting about things you can't change?

- Do you find yourself thinking about something that has happened or could happen to you all of the time? Do you find it difficult to break free from these thoughts, no matter how hard you try?

- Do you get frustrated when things aren't going your way?

- Do you find yourself doing the same things over and over again for no apparent reason?

- Do you seek reassurance from family and friends for these thoughts or acts regularly?

If you answered "yes" to any of the above questions, this innovative and exciting book will give you the chance to restore your peace of mind by following a detailed, step-by-step guide to overcoming obsession.

Beware of Obsession takes the reader on an illuminating trip inside the inner workings of an OCD-affected mind. Readers are then taught how to take a breath, focus inward, and respond rationally to promote healing. By way of multiple tactics, readers learn to tap into millennia-old wisdom drawn from books and combine expansive knowledge with rigorously researched cognitive-behavioral interventions.

Happy Reading!

Obsession
My-mindguide.com

INTRODUCTION

Obsessions are persistent, invasive, involuntary, unreasonable, and anxiety-provoking thoughts. Obsessions can be defined as any concept that meets these five requirements.

When individuals use the term "obsessed" with anything—for example, "Scott is obsessed with dating Julie"—they indicate that Scott thinks about Julie regularly. Perhaps from time to time, thoughts of Julie invade his consciousness. However, I doubt Scott would characterize his feelings about Julie as unreasonable, unconscious, or anxiety-inducing (unless he has a touch of social anxiety or fears rejection). Scott's state is more accurately described as "infatuation." (It's worth noting that the term "to make dumb" originated in the Middle Ages.)

Obsessions must also be distinguished from anxieties, though the distinction is hazier in this case. The critical difference is that obsessions are irrational and do not involve real-world concerns. The obsessive may be aware that the stove is turned off or that they have not unintentionally run over someone, but they must check to feel positive. Additionally, the person with obsessions would want to think about something other than their interest.

Worrying is best characterized as concentrating on one's feelings or issues regarding the future; *rumination*, on the other hand, is best defined as lingering on one's surfaces or difficulties in the past. Worry and thought are not wholly involuntary: when asked if they benefit from worrying or ruminating, most people will respond affirmatively (while admitting that it also does them harm). Individuals suffering from OCD will frequently regard their obsessions as absolutely pointless and will happily give them up in a heartbeat. Worriers tend to have a more difficult time breaking free from their fears.

Finally, it is critical to understand that simply possessing obsessions does not constitute having obsessive-compulsive disorder (OCD). 80 percent of the population experiences sporadic obsessive thoughts. OCD is defined as a disordered fear of obsessions that generates significant suffering and may be accompanied by compulsive behaviors that end the obsessive thinking artificially. In general, the less inclined someone is to have obsessions, the more likely they may occur and progress to OCD. Suppose obsessions are acknowledged as eccentric products of the association cortex and are not elevated in importance. In that case, they will not become dreaded—and so one will be protected from developing OCD in the future.

Obsessive Thoughts – Don't Allow Them to Take Control of Your Life

Obsessive thoughts are a type of anxiety condition in which individuals become trapped in an endless cycle of recurrent thoughts and activities. Individuals who suffer from OCD are troubled by recurrent and stressful thoughts, anxieties, and obsessions that they feel unable to control.

Obsessive thoughts generate anxiety or worry, which creates an urgent need to engage in compulsive rituals or routines. These rituals are conducted in an attempt to prevent or eliminate obsessive thinking. However, these practices are virtually never successful in doing so.

While compulsive conduct may momentarily alleviate obsessive thoughts, the individual must repeat the behavior when the obsessive thoughts return.

The vicious cycle can consume hours and in severe situations, an entire day, interfering with the individual's typical activities and goals. While individuals who have obsessive thoughts are generally aware that their obsessions and compulsions are negatively affecting their life, they cannot manage their thoughts and behaviors without assistance.

What are the factors that contribute to obsessive thoughts?

Although the exact source of obsessive thinking is unknown, various studies have indicated that it is caused by a combination of biological and environmental variables. Additionally, there is evidence that those who have obsessive thoughts suffer from a deficiency of serotonin, a type of neurotransmitter, in their brains. Because this shortage of serotonin can be handed down genetically, obsessive thoughts, like many other mental diseases, can be inherited.

Obsessive thinking may also emerge as a result of persistent drug use or a catastrophic brain injury sustained as a child or adult. Additionally, it can manifest as a side effect of certain prescription and over-the-counter drugs.

Is it possible that certain environmental factors contribute to obsessive thoughts?

Numerous environmental factors can provoke obsessive thinking in persons who are predisposed to acquire the illness. Additionally, these environmental elements may contribute to the aggravation of symptoms. These are the following instances:

- Stress – this can be related to work, relationships, finances, or disease
- Bereavement of a loved one
- Sexual, physical, or emotional abuse
- Residence Situation
- Chronic Substance Abuse

What symptoms indicate obsessive thoughts?

Obsessive-compulsive disorder symptoms differ, as they are grounded in thoughts, and the types of thoughts experienced by individuals vary drastically.

Among the most prevalent obsessive thoughts are the following:

- Fear of germ contamination
- Fear of harboring nefarious intentions
- Fear of embarrassment
- Persistent requirement for precision, cleanliness, or order
- Fear of committing an error
- Excessive doubt and a constant desire for reassurance
- Fear of injuring another

Some of the most common compulsive behaviors are:

- Avoiding handshakes and touching doorknobs
- Consuming food in a particular order

- Constantly inspecting objects, such as door locks or windows
- Amassing objects
- Constantly counting loudly or mentally
- Repetition of particular words, phrases, or prayers
- Frequent bathing, showering, or handwashing
- Constantly arranging objects in a particular order
- Being unable to let go of upsetting words, images, or thoughts
- Repetitive tasks

How are obsessive thoughts treated?

Obsessive thoughts undoubtedly have something to do with the way you think. If the obsessive thoughts are a result of an external stressor, the individual must manage both their ideas and the situation that generated the disorder (e.g., abuse). Often, counseling is necessary to address and resolve these environmental circumstances and the associated thoughts.

Obsessive thinking symptoms vary in severity, and chronic obsessive thinking may require medication to assist the patient in coping until they can learn how to deal with the underlying cause of the problem.

For the majority of persons who suffer from the illness, there is hope since they can naturally break free from their compulsive thoughts. It just requires professional guidance from a program that teaches you how to think positively and how to recognize and avoid the triggers of obsessive thinking. There are plenty of excellent ones available online.

Additionally, learning meditation and inner silence techniques is beneficial. The most critical thing to remember if you have obsessive thoughts is that you can change them and live a healthy life.

Obsession
My-mindguide.com

HOW TO AVOID OBSESSION

The majority of successful people are passionate about their work. This obsession with something can be both exhilarating and gratifying. However, if your thoughts become fixated on a particular person, object, or activity to the point where they impair or disrupt your quality of life, you may have an obsession. This sort of behavioral addiction is manageable by altering one's mentality and routine in such a way that fresh chances present themselves.

Changing Your Mental Attitude

Evaluate your requirements, desires, and objectives. You may be preoccupied because you regard your fixation as an integral aspect of your identity. Instead, you must concentrate on yourself. Separate yourself mentally from your fixation by analyzing how other aspects of your life contribute to your identity. Consider tasks, responsibilities, or jobs that provide you with as much satisfaction as your preoccupation. Is your infatuation with a person, place, or thing motivated by a fantasy or idealized version?

You must first recognize how the fixation has benefited or fulfilled you to begin meeting that need in other ways. For instance, if you are currently in a romantic relationship but are fixated on a coworker who flirts with you, you may need to redirect your attention to reviving the joy experienced with your partner.

Maintain a state of mindfulness. Develop an unjudgmental awareness of yourself and your surroundings. To accomplish this, pay attention to each of your senses while also keeping an eye on your physical or mental state. Consider whether your body feels tense, if you are exhausted, or if you are pleased with your life. Even for little periods, being mindful can help you become more aware of yourself.

Mindfulness can assist you in developing a stronger connection to yourself and others by increasing your empathy and emotional intelligence. It may even prevent you from concentrating negatively on circumstances beyond your control. As such, you'll be able to control your dread or anxiety when stressed.

Redirect your concentration. Consider something else to divert your attention away from your obsessive thoughts. Be gentle with yourself if your attention wanders back to your addiction; simply note the notion, and let it pass as you practice focusing on something else.

Try reading a good book, conversing with a friend, or taking on a new volunteer role to distract yourself. You might also engage in physical activity, such as taking a yoga class or preparing a difficult meal.

Compose a letter to your compulsion. If you find yourself emotionally drained as a result of chronic obsessing, you need to reconnect with your emotional needs. An excellent method is writing a letter to your fixation, explaining why you were drawn to it and laying out the role it has played in your life—along with the emotions elicited by your fixation. Additionally, explain to your preoccupation why it has become concerning or why it is giving you trouble.

Acquainting yourself with your emotional requirements will enable you to begin addressing them without relying on your fixation.

Put an end to your compulsive thoughts. You may be continually fixated on something. To prevent these obsessive thoughts from interfering with your life, convince yourself that you will obsess only at particular periods of the day. Put it off for now and convince yourself that you can obsess later. You may discover that your mind relaxes sufficiently, allowing you to forget about your obsession.

For instance, if you find yourself obsessing about something while out with your friends, remind yourself to enjoy the present, recalling that you can always obsess afterward.

Developing New Prospects

Determine a way to overcome your obsession. If you're fixated on a particular challenge or issue, attempt to resolve it. Create a list of alternatives so that you feel as though you have choices. If you're having difficulty seeing alternative solutions, speak with those who have encountered a problem similar to the one you're attempting to resolve. Other individuals may be able to provide you with a fresh perspective that could help you to resolve your issue.

For instance, perhaps you've been fretting over a means to maintain your fitness level during a life transition. Your obstacle may be scheduling your morning run while still being able to drop off your new infant at daycare. You may speak with another new parent or offer to swap childcare duties so you can work out.

Establish a support system. You may feel separated from friends and family as a result of your obsession with something or someone. Re-establish contact with friends, relatives, and coworkers who can assist you in explaining your predicament. Speaking with someone can assist you in determining the underlying cause of your fixation, and having a support network in place can help alleviate tension.

By way of example, if you're obsessed with an ex following a breakup, speak to a friend or family member. Discussing your obsession with a buddy may help you recognize that you're infatuated since your ex was the first person to take you seriously in a relationship.

Experiment with new experiences. It's all too easy to fall into a rut of obsessing over something if you're not constantly challenging yourself. If you've been intending to take up a new activity or enroll in a class, now is the time. Not only can focusing on a new task or talent divert your attention away from your fixation, but you may also meet new people or discover something new about yourself.

Meeting new people and adopting fresh ways of thinking can assist you in overcoming your fixation. You may discover that you no longer crave the object of your fixation. For instance, you may not be as concerned about a missed work chance if you learn a new trade that you genuinely enjoy.

Make a good difference in the lives of others. You may be so preoccupied with everything going on in your life that you entirely disregard the lives of your friends, family members, and/or community members. Make contact with those who may require your assistance as well. Not only will people appreciate it, but you'll also come to know that life is more than your passion. For instance, you could tutor at a school, volunteer at a soup kitchen, or transport an elderly relative to the shop.

Developing New Habits

Keep your exposure to your fixation to a minimum. If you're infatuated with something, such as video games or television, gradually minimize your time spent on it. If you're obsessed with someone, keep your contact with them to a minimum too. Reducing your addiction can help you become more self-sufficient and carefree. For instance, if you're limiting your contact with someone, remember to include time spent on social media. Avoid frequent texting, image-swapping, and phone calls.

Maintain a busy schedule. When you're pressed for time, it's easy to lose track of what's bugging you. Preoccupy your mind to avoid obsessing. Along with exploring new activities, you may also catch up on duties you've been meaning to complete while maintaining contact with your support network and devoting time to yourself.

You may discover that a significant portion of your time was previously spent obsessing. Consider the tasks you've put off and finally complete them. For instance, you may get a haircut or meet up with pals for a drink that you've been putting off.

Assume accountability. It's all too simple to turn your passion into someone else's issue. However, rather than fretting about something you assume is someone else's fault, simply own up to it. Accepting responsibility will assist you in gaining control of your thoughts. Only you have authority over your ideas, and you alone are capable of ceasing to obsess. For instance, if a coworker received a promotion that you were vying for, refrain from blaming the colleague and obsessing about it. Instead, accept your colleague's superior qualifications, and strive to improve yourself.

Spend time with a social group that is dissimilar to your own. If you have an obsession with something—whether it's a drug, video game, or a person—chances are your buddies help you to maintain that obsession. To *quit* obsessing, you should be in an environment where you're not tempted to do so and where those around you don't bring it up. You may wish to spend your spare time in a different hangout location and with individuals who don't enable you, even if this means breaking up with specific buddies.

Are all of your acquaintances members of this culture? Then, you may be forced to rely on family members. Take this opportunity to reconnect with folks with whom you've fallen out of touch recently. You might reintroduce yourself to persons you've been missing in your life.

Take a break and enjoy yourself. It's stressful to be fixated on something or someone. Take a break from the worry and engage in a pleasant activity. You may luxuriate in a bubble bath, practice deep breathing, or simply relax with a glass of wine and a book. The aim is to do something you enjoy that also serves as a stress reliever. If you're having difficulty relaxing due to obsessive thoughts, consider listening to a guided imagery CD or reading an anxiety-relief script.

Obssession

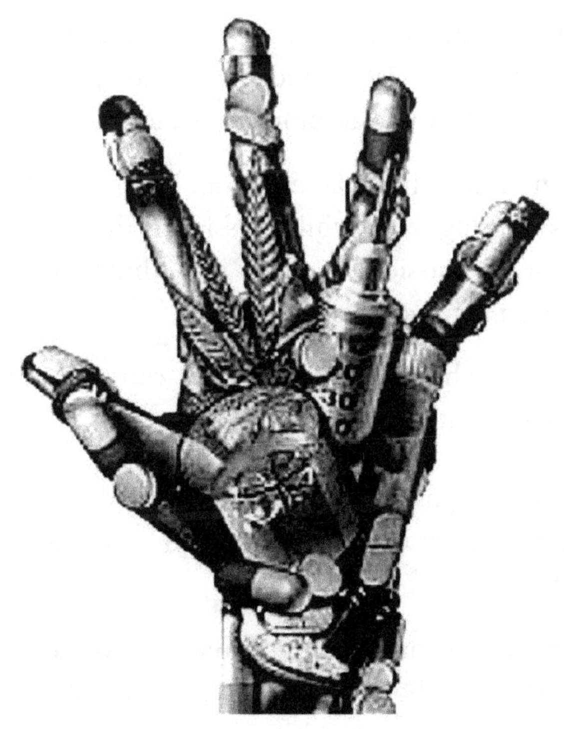

WHAT IS PASSION AND WHAT DOES HAVING PASSION MEAN?

I frequently use the term *passion* interchangeably with *determination*, *conviction*, and *love*. Passion is a powerful desire that can motivate you to accomplish extraordinary things.

Passion is an actionable emotion. Without action, passion produces nothing worthwhile. Passion is the ignitor of action. When you are passionate about something, you will always love it—even if you despise it.

Therefore, what is passion? How can you identify your passion and put it to use?

What exactly is passion?

A desire that is motivated by passion will produce the best results in life.

I enjoy ice-skating but lack the willpower to persevere through shattered bones and hospital stays. That is why I am not as good as I am capable of being. I lack enthusiasm for it. Passion can carry you through difficult times because you are unconcerned about what it takes to improve. We all have the potential to create the life we desire. The key to living the dream lies in our passions and the work we undertake as a result of them.

How do you determine your area of interest?
Finding your passion is a journey in and of itself. Do not be discouraged if you do not feel as though you know yet. Continue to experiment with new things. It will come regardless of whether you have to construct it. If you discover your passion or are on the verge of discovering it, don't give up!

What if you are aware of your passion but do nothing about it? This is the primary difficulty with passion. You can have all the enthusiasm in the world for something, but if you never act on it, your enthusiasm is meaningless.

Perhaps you have a good career that pays the bills but doesn't allow you to pursue your passion fully. You're fearful of what will happen if you alter the status quo. Yes, change is frightening, but it's only when we leave our comfort zone that we discover what we've been missing.

Your life is entirely up to you, so don't accept the bare minimum simply because it is functioning right now.

Unless you push yourself, you will never know what you are capable of.

However, even if you pursue your passion, you will encounter failures and other roadblocks. That cannot be allowed to affect you. It happens to everyone who pursues their ideal life. Abe Lincoln was driven by a passionate desire to construct a great country. Do you believe he was deterred from doing so by a few setbacks? Allow no impediments to bring you down.

14 Incredible Things That Happen When You Follow Your Passion

While society would have you believe that following your passion is irresponsible and dumb, we're going to highlight fourteen incredible things that happen when you do.

1. Enhanced Self-Belief

It's a little-known fact that everyone desires acceptance for who they are. Nonetheless, not everyone is at ease expressing who they are. When you disregard others' opinions and pursue your passion, you will develop a greater capacity for self-expression.

Oftentimes, when you're not following your passion, you're living the life you believe people would accept. When you succumb to the pressures of society, your friends, and your family, your confidence will suffer. This is largely because you are coerced into doing something uninteresting to you.

There is almost certainly a reason for this, and when you don't work within your range of talents and interests, your performance will suffer.

2. Decreased Stress

Adults' primary source of stress is work-related, which has been linked to higher risks of heart attack, hypertension, and other diseases.

Allow me to begin by dispelling the myth that all stress is harmful. Those who pursue their passions and those who do not will experience stress in equal measure. The distinction lies in the type of stress encountered.

Those that follow their passions have an internal motivation that contributes to their situation's balance. As a result, they will almost certainly encounter stressful situations regularly. Consider the following scenario: you have three critical tasks that must be completed on the same day. As a result, you feel anxious throughout the day.

Those who are not living their passion are frequently dissatisfied with their jobs and find them burdensome daily. They are stressed by the act of rising, dressing, and driving to work. They dread Mondays and long for Fridays.

3. Fulfillment in Your Work

As we mentioned previously, nothing is more tiring than "working to survive." You feel trapped because you have bills to pay and your employer provides the funds to pay the expenses.

Even if there is some uncertainty surrounding your passion, you cannot overstate the importance of enjoying your work.

Pursuing your passion will ensure that you are fulfilled in your work. You won't feel compelled to listen to podcasts or audiobooks while working (trying to fill that void). Instead of *planning* to live your passion, you will experience the delight of actually living it. There is nothing more gratifying than fulfilling your calling.

4. Expertise in Work-Life Balance

There is a proverb that states that if you live your passion, you will no longer require a work-life balance. The premise is that a work-life balance is necessary only when one's job is depleting you.

When you follow your passion, you maintain a permanent state of equilibrium in your life. Because you would do it for free, your work doesn't feel like a job.

Consider the possibility of wishing you could work because you appreciate what you do. That is precisely what will occur if you pursue your passion.

5. Fewer Regrets Later in Life

In the end, the majority of individuals will regret not what they did but what they didn't do.

Consider how different your life would be if you pursued all of your desires and passions. Consider what would happen if you bumped into that individual and were forced to explain why you didn't pursue your interest wholeheartedly. This is the real-world dialogue that the majority of people have when it's almost too late.

Take a chance and bet on yourself. Even if it doesn't work out exactly as planned, you will benefit from the experience.

6. Personal Development

The majority of people don't live their passions due to the uncertainty that surrounds them. You may have reservations about your financial, professional, or even emotional success.

Occasionally, you're correct in your assessment. This is not to say that you should accept this situation and take no action to change it. Rather, spend some time honing the skills necessary to pursue your interest.

If you still wish to be an astronaut, you can pursue a career as a rocket scientist. You can continue practicing and pursuing your pilot's license if you wish to remain a pilot.

Determine whatever talents you need to learn to live your passion, and then take the necessary measures.

7. Positive Attraction

At times, you may fear that your passion will not be adequately received by others. The problem with living a life that is less than honest is that you will attract the wrong individuals.

When you live your life and pursue your passions, you will attract individuals who share your values.

To be honest, pursuing your passion is likely to irritate *someone*. People dislike change, and when you change, your relationships may suffer.

However, don't let this be a hindrance. Your growth is contingent upon your commitment to pursue the beliefs necessary to accomplish your objective.

8. Expand Your Comfort Zone

Avoid the trap of assuming that you must give up everything to pursue your passion. These types of restricting ideas prevent the majority of individuals from ever embarking on a path to changing their lives.

Indeed, you don't have to abandon everything to begin again. Allow yourself to gradually widen your comfort zone and experiment with new activities. You can continue living your current life while also chasing new opportunities.

As you gain confidence in your abilities to pursue your passion, you may gradually devote more time to it. You will soon be all-in and embracing life to the fullest.

9. Show Gratitude

It is true that you may and should always feel grateful. There is always something in your life to be grateful for. Even if you experience a flat tire on your way home from work, you still have a vehicle.

Similarly, you should constantly be grateful for the opportunity to work. Nonetheless, there is little doubt that you will feel more appreciative if you spend each day engaged in an activity that you are enthusiastic about. You can find yourself looking forward to waking up each morning since it means another day fulfilling your life's purpose.

10. Re-establish Contact with Your Inner Self

Once upon a time, you felt liberated. You felt as though you could accomplish anything and that anything was possible.

When you begin to live your passion, you are almost certainly reconnecting with the activities you enjoyed as a child. By pausing for a moment and rediscovering the things you enjoyed before society dictated what you should love, you can reclaim a piece of yourself.

Reminisce about your childhood delights and keep track of the activities you enjoyed. You, like me, may discover that you enjoy putting puzzles together. This may reflect your analytical personality and explain why you are so passionate about putting things together and solving difficulties. Whatever it is, take a minute to recover the "authentic self" that was compelled to "grow up."

11. Kinder Person

Your passion is almost certain to benefit a large number of individuals. You believe there is something wrong with the world and that you can help fix it. There is no question that if more people followed their passions, the world would be a better place.

When you are living your passion, you will experience a sense of calm and joy that will permeate your interactions with others. Perhaps you've heard the adage "hurt people, harm people." This suggests that the person who is ineffective at your job is most likely struggling with a personal issue.

When you follow your passion, you will feel fulfilled and at peace with the world, and you will be more empathetic toward others.

12. Unleash Your Imagination

The thing with living a life devoid of enthusiasm is that you are almost certainly following a well-worn road. In life, security is frequently synonymous with the absence of innovation.

When you deviate from the route of least resistance and pursue your passion, you must tap into your creativity to succeed. You will be sailing into unfamiliar waters throughout your life, which can be daunting. However, this is where the magic occurs.

When you come face to face with an impediment that stands between you and your passion, you must have faith in yourself that you will overcome it.

13. Substitute a Different Narrative

You have an inner voice that informs you of who you are, what you are capable of accomplishing, and what you deserve. At times, you may have conflicting emotions about pursuing your interest. On the one hand, you're appreciative of the life you've been given and satisfied with everything that comes with it. Alternatively, you are driven by a passionate urge to pursue your passion and take a chance.

By gaining knowledge of the restricting story you are telling yourself (e.g., I'm not good enough; I should be content with the job I currently have, etc.), you will be better equipped to alter your narrative.

Your new narrative will be based on the realization that you may pursue your passion without being ungrateful or unappreciative of the life you now enjoy.

14. Overcome Your Fears

Fear breeds delays, which suffocate your ambition to follow your passion.

Avoid the urge to justify maintaining the status quo until you have more experience, time, and influence. There is always room for improvement. If you succumb to your fears, they will only develop.

By following your passion, you will have overcome your fears. Remember, while it is acceptable to be fearful, it's *not* acceptable to let that dread paralyze your efforts.

What about humanity's passion?

The concept of passion also applies to individuals. Avoid the typical mistake of believing you love someone but doing nothing about it. Consider this: Is it worth it for me to give up my pride to sustain a relationship? How about being selfless and foregoing time or comfort? If you're unable to do so, it's either not true love or you need to make some changes.

Often, I believe, we need to remind ourselves of our values and act appropriately. It's all too easy to let family connections deteriorate due to pride. Of course, you claim to love your family, but do you attend your brother's school performance if you despise plays?

Intimate interactions are no different. Are you only fond of them when it's convenient? Genuine love necessitates sacrifice and effort. You persevere through the difficult times because you care about them and understand that any passion worth pursuing will encounter setbacks. Regrettably, many people lack an understanding of what it means to be passionate about someone. This is why divorce rates are so high and families are frequently torn apart by ill-advised turmoil.

Pursuing a passion requires both vulnerability and effort. However, I guarantee that the eventual result of such efforts will be the most fulfilling part of your life. The flexibility and ease of burden are two of the most exciting aspects of living your passion.

Consider for a second how your life would be different if you followed your passion. Then, stop simply thinking! You must go out and begin living it.

Regardless of how minor the modification is, you will begin to notice the benefits indicated. Once you begin to notice the benefits, there will be no stopping you.

Finding Your Core Passion

Unhappiness comes from attempting to be who we are not; the journey of life is to gain clarity about who you are . . . so that you can be your authentic self.

Ever wonder why they say “play to your strengths” in every aspect of life? The adage comes from a belief that every individual has something unique about them that sets them apart from everyone else.

Finding one’s core purpose and managing to enhance and polish it not only makes for a happier and healthier life but guarantees success.

Theory of Morph

An interesting philosophy behind the concept of the core is the Theory of Morph. The theory states that the potential of a person is determined while they’re still in their mother’s womb as a fetus.

The theory elaborates that the core of a person depends upon which part of the fetus is foremost formed. This could be the head, torso, or limbs.

Babies that first develop the head (nervous system, skin, nails, etc.) are known as ectomorphs. They are said to have large foreheads and are essentially known to be intellectuals and prefer to deal with matters of the logic and brain.

These people are thinkers, capable of analyzing complex data and arriving at conclusive inferences.

Some babies develop the torso (stomach, intestines, and heart) first. These are called endomorphs and tend to be broader or round around the middle. They are known to possess great emotional intelligence and have the ability to empathize with a variety of people. They understand human dynamics and can solve conflicts easily.

Babies that first develop their limbs are called mesomorphs, and their intelligence is purely physical. They have perfect hand-eye coordination and are envied for their physique and abundant energy. Their forte lies in anything where physical strength and operational decision-making are required.

This theory doesn't imply we need to ask our doctors how we were born. It simply stresses the fact that we all possess a specific trait that helps us excel in whatever we undertake.

Coming to the most important question . . . What is *your* core? It is a specific purpose with which you really connect on a deeper level and which comes about effortlessly.

A core purpose will absorb you completely to the extent that you are oblivious of all that is around you.

Only when you use something you are great at and apply it to what you care about with relentless passion does the magic happen and the adventure ultimately begin. In short, your physical, emotional, intellectual, and spiritual being come together in that activity.

I believe you have inside you a core genius—one thing that you love to do and do so well that you hardly feel like doing anything else. It's effortless for you and a whole lot of fun. And if you could make money doing it, you'd make it your life's work.

Successful people believe this, too. That's why they put their core genius first. They focus on it and delegate everything else to other people on their team.

Identify Your Core

When we say "play your strengths," the implication is to unleash that core competency within you, which will take your performance to a higher level.

Individuals dealing with their core are seen at their best, they derive immense pleasure, satisfaction, and fun not known to them any other way.

Obssession

OBSESSING OVER OBSESSIONS

Obsession. Such a strong term. A word that conjures up images of scary men enamored with the girl they can't have. Photos of the creepy girl who becomes obsessed with stalking someone she has a crush on—images of evil men consumed by the desire to accumulate treasure at all costs.

Yes, obsession is a strong word with negative implications in general. Often, the wicked are portrayed as being driven in this manner, while the righteous are portrayed as the stereotypical saint battling evil's devotion. However, obsession is rarely exposed for what it truly is.

A large number of us wouldn't believe ourselves to be the detestable man or frightening woman who plague our musings to the point of madness. However, if we're completely candid, we would become acquainted with those who are the force of good in the face of such evil. We're looking into the depths of our eyes—into the abyss of our soul. Yes . . . there it is: the truth. Everyone has suffered from some form of fixation. Some are more enamored with it than others. It manifests itself obviously in some people's lives, while others conceal it in their closets. However, when we open our eyes, there it is, looking back at us with those haunting, determined eyes—that unending thirst that leaves us dehydrated regardless of how much we drink.

How to Make a Connection with Divine Energy and Your Superior Self

The divine self, or higher self, is a belief shared by Hindus and adherents of New-Age thinking. According to these beliefs, the divine self is the self that exists on a higher plane than the soul; it is present in every human being who has ever been born. It is the Universe's true essence that resides within you, the source of all light and life within you, and your true reason for living.

Your divine essence is what propels you forward and inspires you to wonder. The spiritual path of the soul light at the center of your being has chosen to incarnate at this moment. It is constantly aware and has been thinking since you began to exist in this lifetime and previous lifetimes. The body and physical realm in which we live are believed to be merely a vehicle for the higher self.

If you've ever encountered synchronicities in your life, which are instances of coincidences that are too strange to be coincidental, you may be on the verge of connecting with your higher self.

According to the same beliefs, the soul is more closely related to the personality and serves as a conduit between the individual and her divine self until she can immediately experience and realize her divine self as who she is.

11 Ways to Connect with Your Soul's Higher Self

Every man is a disguised deity, a fooled god.

—Ralph Waldo Emerson

Throughout history, the higher self has been variously referred to as the inner self, soul, Christ-consciousness, beloved, Buddha-nature, and spirit. Whatever name we use for this essential inner Core, it is our most Divine essence.

Despite our familiarity with these notions, many of us have difficulty comprehending the higher self and its function in our lives. In other words, how can we translate this subject from an abstract intellectual concept to a tangible emotion?

The following routines and practices may assist you in reconnecting with your higher self:

1. Acquaint yourself with the face of your higher self
What does your sacred self-resemble or look like? You may wish to assist yourself with this by using visualization, inner traveling, or self-hypnosis. Although your Higher Self transcends all names and forms, it is beneficial to have a visual representation to assist the human mind.

2. In contact with your higher self? What does it feel like?
For instance, what sensations visit your body during a mystical encounter or a spontaneous contact with this deeper aspect of yourself? How do you feel in your chest, abdomen, head, and body as a whole? Additionally, you can connect with your intuition to assist you in answering this issue. As the voice of your soul/higher self, your intuition allows direct access to this timeless element of you. Pay attention to how your intuition speaks to you. Is it a gentle murmur? Perhaps it is an inner sense of peace, tranquility, compassion, or profound knowledge.

3. What message(s) does your higher self-wish to communicate with you?

You may choose to investigate automatic writing, dream interpretation, and even the usage of oracle cards to connect with your higher self's messages. Additionally, you can increase your body's awareness and use visceral mindfulness to tune in to the present moment's direction. Meditation is another effective method of connecting with your higher self's understanding.

4. Schedule daily time for stillness and reflection

Begin with a daily minimum of ten minutes. You might use this time to meditate or take in the beauty of nature and existence. What emotions or thoughts are you experiencing at the moment? You may choose to keep track of them in a journal. Learn more about journaling.

5. Determine what you can relinquish or let go of

One of the primary reasons we have difficulty connecting with our higher selves is that we have excessive mental and emotional baggage. What needs to be relinquished or eliminated from your life? How can you increase your practice of letting go? Introspection and examination of the beliefs, values, assumptions, and conditions that contribute to your sense of separation and dissatisfaction are of utmost importance.

6. When it comes to self-acceptance and love, what can you do to increase your own and others' self-worth?

Your heart is opened by love, and your heart is a direct conduit to your soul. What could be a more potent method of rediscovering your true nature? The more love you feel, the more expansive life becomes and the more fully you may embody your higher self. Self-love is a critical component of experiencing your True Nature. Consider the following: "What within me requires the loving arms of compassion and self-forgiveness right now?"

7. For one day, practice non-resistance ("going with the flow")
Allow everything to unfold naturally, including your thoughts, feelings, and external events. At the very least, give it a day. What are your feelings? The more we reject existence, the more our dualistic brains become imprisoned. Non-resistance doesn't imply being a doormat or a pushover (it is necessary to establish limits and say no). Instead, non-resistance is a way of life. It respects reality—and the more attached we are to reality, the easier it is to connect with our higher selves.

8. Acquaint yourself with who (or what) your spirit guide is
Spirit guides are strong entities who assist us in connecting with our inherent truth, courage, wisdom, and love. It makes no difference whether you believe they are archetypes or actual autonomous energies: they can assist you in connecting with your higher self by guiding you toward rediscovering who you truly are.

9. Locate your soul's home
Each of us has at least one soul location on earth. A soul place is a unique location or location where we feel a sense of belonging, empowerment, and energetic refreshment. By calming and slowing down your nervous system and stimulating introspection and mindfulness, finding your soul space will assist you in connecting with your true self.

10. Experiment with mirror work

What do you sense when you gently gaze into your own eyes in a mirror and invoke the presence of your soul? What do you encounter? Indeed, the eyes serve as windows into the Soul. Consider whether you can gently push through the voices of self-judgment that arise naturally when engaging in this activity and connect with your inner source. This is a highly effective and practical reconnection method with your higher nature. Continue reading to learn more about mirror work.

11. Maintain an awareness of the current moment

Awakening to your true nature can only occur in the present moment. This is the secret transmitted through ancient traditions and spiritual teachings: Paradise is within you, and the Kingdom of Heaven is now.

The obstacle we encounter is the monkey mind, continuously scurrying around, attempting to transport us to some distant future location. However, life's splendor and ultimate compassion are such that you don't have to search for your higher self/soul in the future: it's already within you!

Regrettably, most of us struggle to accept this basic yet essential reality. Our minds have such a powerful hold on us that we can scarcely remain motionless for two seconds without wriggling and attempting to ignore our feelings. This is why it's critical to combine spirituality and psychology. We require psychology to assist us in untangling our inner knots, and we need spirituality to loosen the mind.

Establish a daily meditation practice to communicate with your higher self. Examine several meditation techniques (such as breath awareness, open awareness, body scanning, and self-inquiry) and determine which ones work best for you. Occasionally, a combination of strategies is the most effective. If you require assistance, consider using a free meditation tool like *Calm*, *Headspace*, or *InsightTimer*.

The Benefits of Connecting with Your Higher Self

The following are some of the unavoidable benefits of rediscovering your true nature. Indeed, depending on the strength of the meeting, I prefer to refer to these "benefits" as "semi-permanent to permanent transformations of being":

- Significantly reduced or eliminated anxiety
- Decreased or eliminated depression
- Receptivity and openness to life
- Imagination and inspiration
- Increased intuitive abilities and spiritual/personal gifts
- A greater capacity for tolerance and forbearance
- Loss of fear of death
- Formation of a mystical perspective on life
- Development of unwavering love for oneself and others

These "benefits" are a drop in the bucket in terms of experiencing your higher self, though! Due to the unique and intimate nature of the experience, we all experience different advantages to varying degrees.

The "Higher" Self is Not Accurate

Indeed, any title applied to "that-powerful-presence-within-us" is incorrect, as it simultaneously transcends and absorbs all labels. On an absolute level, our true nature is simply what it is; it exists beyond time, duality, and cognition.

However, it is beneficial for the human mind to refer to that powerful presence inside us as the higher self, as it doesn't actually feel "higher" than the ego (and so it is in a sense). However, it's not all spirituality, and we must be cautious not to equate spirituality with the ascending, transcendent path.

Remember that true spirituality, your true nature, covers all aspects of life. It is present in both mundane and ecstatic and wonderful moments. It is present while cleaning dirty pans in the sink or staring at the stars.

While terms like *higher self*, *Buddha-nature*, and *soul* are useful, they are ultimately restrictive. Who you are is far more than an abstract concept. Bear this in mind as you endeavor to rediscover the truth about who you really are.

Obsessive-Compulsive Disorder's History

Obsessive-compulsive disorder has a history dating back thousands of years. As far as we are aware, OCD has existed for as long as man has. It has a significant impact on a vast number of people worldwide. It is not race-specific, and indeed, other animals also have it. After all, animals too experience worries and, like humans, they can form habits out of those fears. Numerous variables can predispose someone to acquire a significant problem with OCD behavior. Fortunately, it is not required to pinpoint precisely what caused it in the individual; if the common reasons are addressed, and the individual is educated on how to refocus their attention away from OCD thoughts, they will improve with patience and persistence.

I am aware that there is nothing particularly seductive about that response, but that is how it is. The history and causes of obsessive-compulsive disorder remain unknown. Regrettably, most practitioners do not grasp it well enough to be of considerable assistance to their clients. I genuinely feel that you must have gone through it yourself to be of true assistance. The greatest way to learn about something is to learn from someone who has gone through it themselves. That is not to imply that someone who has researched it extensively cannot assist you; rather, you may find the process easier if you work with someone who has personally experienced what you are experiencing.

While OCD may be universal, closer examination reveals that each individual is unique. It's like snowflakes in this sense; from a distance, they appear the same, yet upon closer examination, we discover that no two snowflakes are identical. This, I believe, is a tribute to our God's majesty and inventiveness. Most persons with OCD are furious with God and bitter about life, becoming depressed. I sincerely want to caution you to recognize that if you focus on the negative aspects of your life, you will experience more of the same. Following the same principle, if you focus on the positive aspects of your life and show thankfulness to God for them, you will attract more of the same—and be much happier as a result!

If you alter your perspective on things, your viewing objects will also alter. If you view your life as abysmal, that is how you will experience it. However, if you view your life as fantastic, you will have a wonderful experience. Thus, regardless of your history with obsessive-compulsive disorder, you now have an option to be joyful. It's important to remember that, like you and me, people cannot be conscious of their surroundings because of mental illnesses. Do not sit and lament, "Oh poor me!" Rather, consider, "I am glad that I have the ability and the strength to conquer this obstacle!"

Obssession

THE DOWNSIDE OF OBSESSION

At its worst, obsession acts as an iron mask that restricts our vision to a single object—or, to use another metaphor, as a massive tidal wave that crashes through our minds and drowns out all other worries. We may develop an obsession with a person, a place, a goal, or a subject—but in all cases, preoccupation results in the same thing: addiction.

Obsession, like all addictions, is initially alluring. It satisfies us, and what a sense of comfort that is! (especially if we felt empty before). Even if we don't feel empty, preoccupation gives us a sense of strength, capability, and purpose.

However, like with all addictions, fixation unbalances us over time. We frequently begin to overlook aspects of our lives that we should not. If allowed to become excessively consuming, fixation causes us to devalue critical aspects of our lives and to tolerate their deterioration, if not complete collapse. Even if our lives remain balanced, if the object of our devotion is taken from us, we are distraught, frequently thinking we have lost our only shot at happiness.

How to Control an Obsession

The key is to channel our obsessions productively, manage them so that they don't control us, and reap the benefits of fixation without succumbing to their negative consequences. The following tactics may be beneficial in accomplishing this:

1. Divert your attention at varying intervals

Using the force of will to subdue an obsession is similar to combating worry by denying it exists: it rarely works and frequently makes it worse. For better results, find something attractive and delightful to divert your attention away from your addiction and give you a break from it. This will serve as a reminder on an emotional level that other aspects of life remain significant. Read a fascinating novel, watch an interesting film, or lend a hand to a friend in need. Engage in an activity that takes you out of your brain.

2. Complete a job that will assist you in putting your fixation behind you

Sometimes a passion enslaves us and refuses to let go merely because we haven't completed it. Perhaps we haven't updated a book chapter, haven't finalized travel arrangements, or haven't asked out someone on whom we have a crush. Declare to yourself that you will take a break once you accomplish the next milestone. Often, taking a significant stride forward in some way allows you to disengage from addiction and replenish your batteries momentarily. And when you do, return your attention to another area of your life that has been neglected.

3. Maintain a laser-like focus on your larger purpose

Discovering and accepting a life mission will protect you from the idea that your life is pointless. And if you can care about a purpose that offers joy to others or alleviates their pain, you'll find yourself more solidly anchored, erect, and balanced when a tsunami of obsessive thoughts threatens to sweep you away.

4. Develop a grounding practice

Chant. Meditate. Consider taking up karate or dancing. Do something physical in a new environment to engage a different section of your mind that isn't consumed by your preoccupation.

5. Pay attention to what others say

If close friends and family members express concern about your obsession, they are usually correct. Keep an open mind to these messages.

I'm not proposing that we should intend to annihilate fixation; rather, I'm contending that we should look to oversee it. Our power to control our emotions is limited, but not our ability to control them. We can make our obsessions work for us rather than against us. And we can develop the ability to let them go when the moment is right.

How to Put an End to Obsession

Our capacity for thought and reflection on our experiences sets us apart from most other creatures. It enables us to predict difficulties and make plans. Additionally, it enables us to understand and impart meaning to the past.

For many of us, the issue emerges when we cannot switch off our thinking minds. A part of us feels that by fixating on an issue, we might resolve it and free ourselves. Yet, our mind is capable of replaying a problem or event indefinitely without ever resolving it or seeing things more clearly.

We all face difficulties; hardship is a natural part of life. However, a propensity to obsess over our problems can predispose us to worry and sadness. We might become so absorbed in our thoughts that we miss the beauty and joy of life, as well as the calm clarity that comes from being present—a friend's smile, raindrops on the leaves outside the window, the way the setting sun sets the clouds on fire.

Just as it took time to develop the habit of overthinking, overcoming it will require some work. To kick you off, here are a few ideas:

- The next time you find yourself brooding compulsively, pause and ask yourself: What do I require right now? Is it necessary for me to eat something? Is it necessary for me to walk around or go outside? Should I contact an old friend? Recognizing when you are contemplating and refocusing your attention retrains your mind to relax and avoid being drawn into a vortex of your thoughts.

- Snap yourself out of it. Secure your wrist with a rubber band. When you become aware of yourself ruminating, snap the rubber band and redirect your attention.

- Assume a comfortable position and follow these directions for breathing: Inhale for four counts, hold for four counts, then exhale for four counts. This should be repeated for at least five minutes. Breathing nourishes the body and diverts the mind's attention.

- Pull Over. This strategy originates from Therese J. Borchard, who developed an online guide to conquering obsessions. Consider that you are driving a car. Consider heading over to the roadside at whatever point you see yourself pushing. Then inquire: Is there anything I need to correct? Is there anything I should alter? Is there anything else I can do to make peace with the situation about which I'm contemplating? If the answer is "no," then abandon the preoccupation and resume your journey. This is a technique for teaching yourself to focus on the things you can alter and let go of the rest.

- Disconnect from your intellect and reconnect with your senses. When we are alone with our thoughts, we tend to overthink things. Activities that take you out of your head and into the real world can assist in breaking the cycle. Take a walk, for example, and note anything blue or green. Bike along the river trail and enjoy the breeze on your face. Prepare a dish that you've never made before using a recipe. Light an incense stick and play some soothing music.

- Become acquainted with and practice meditation. One straightforward technique is to follow the stream of sounds as they rise and fall in real-time. Allow distracting thoughts to pass and return your attention to the stream of sounds. When we become fixated on an issue or the past, it can feel like we're being held hostage by a force greater than ourselves. However, building a strong habit of systematically letting go of your ideas will enable you to reach a more spacious frame of mind, even in the face of adversity.

Thinking is an amazing tool that enables us to plan for the future, predict issues, and *resolve* our biggest problems. However, to live a balanced existence and avoid wasting time worrying, we must learn to deal with our obstacles and take in our surroundings. Often, the most profound insights occur when we stop thinking and allow our thoughts to be open to a richer stream of experience.

9 Signs of Obsessive Love

Have you ever heard of "obsessive love disorder"?

When we are attracted to someone, be it a guy or a girl, it is natural to have persistent thoughts about that person; it's natural to want to spend every waking moment with that individual.

A healthy relationship relies on these thoughts, which encourage partners to spend as much time together as possible. These ideas and sentiments develop into greater respect, maturity, and commitment with time.

However, if we believe the person we're attracted to isn't truly interested in us, unrequited love can occasionally create obsessive thoughts—which can be atrocious, as your fanatical considerations may hold you back from advancing throughout everyday life.

HEALTHY RELATIONSHIPS

VERSUS

UNHEALTHY RELATIONSHIPS

IT'S IMPORTANT TO KNOW THE DIFFERENCE BETWEEN A HEALTHY RELATIONSHIP AND UNHEALTHY ONE, ESPECIALLY IN COLLEGE. HERE ARE SOME CHARACTERISTICS TO HELP YOU DISTINGUISH:

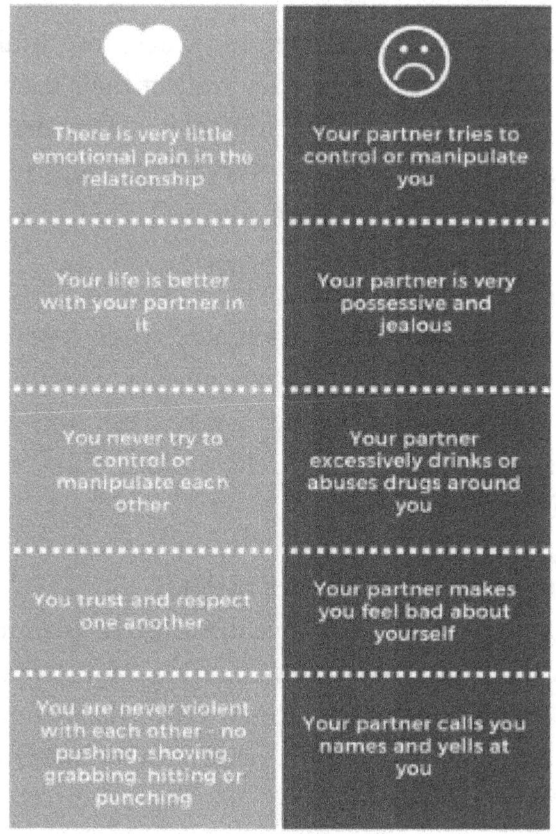

For more information, you can visit: Iona College Counseling Center or the UTEP Counseling Center

If you're wondering whether your intense feelings for a (prospective) partner are unhealthy, it's critical to determine whether you're exhibiting symptoms of obsessive love. The following are nine frequently occurring signs:

#1. Constantly Considering the Individual

Someone suffering from obsessive love usually wants to spend an excessive amount of time with the other person, to the point that they're always thinking about them and acting in ways that connect them to the other person.

Because obsessive lovers spend so much time thinking about the object of their devotion, they neglect their friends, family, and work, resulting in a low quality of life. They may withdraw from recreational activities or other connections to the extent that they cannot function normally.

#2. Feelings of Unworthiness

As humans, we are most vulnerable when we fall in love. Falling in love entails accepting the chance of being abandoned or rejected. If you don't believe you're deserving of that love, you'll feel insecure in your relationship, thus continuously fearful of being wounded.

#3. Feeling Possessive (They're MINE!)

If you suffer from obsessive love disorder, you cannot bear the thought of this other person considering dating anybody other than you. Additionally, you don't want other people to view this person as a viable object of adoration since you believe they're yours and yours alone.

This may result in jealous outbursts directed at strangers or close friends who engage with your passion. Additionally, it might result in incorrect conclusions about an interaction between this person and another, resulting in potential embarrassment for overreacting.

#4. The Irrational Need to "Defend" the Object of One's Obsessive Love

You pretend to want to protect the individual from harm, but in reality, you isolate them from the rest of the world. You could attempt to minimize their social interactions by telling this person that their friends and family are toxic. Creating boundaries for them in the name of "their own good" is a form of control that results from obsession.

#5. Jealousy When You Witness This Individual Engage with Members of the Opposite Sex

This is the result of your possessive feelings toward this person. You don't want anyone to believe this individual is available or that they could have feelings for anyone but you. Additionally, you don't want the object of your passion to find someone they believe will be a better match for them than you.

#6. Intolerance of Rejection

If the other person walks out on you during a fight, hangs up on you, or otherwise rejects you, you may have a strong reaction. Any indication of rejection from this person drives you into a state of terror, believing you may lose them forever. You're incapable of accepting defeat or rejection.

#7. Repeated Phone Calls and Text Messages

Not only do you need to keep an eye on this individual throughout the day, but you also want to stay on their mind continually. Interacting with them via texts and phone conversations enables you to keep track of their whereabouts throughout the day and ensure that they're paying attention to you.

Suppose you don't receive a response for an extended period. In that case, you are likely to become agitated and frustrated and jump to the worst possible conclusions, believing they are with another person or doing something behind your back.

#8. Reduced Interaction with Family and Friends as a Result of Preoccupation with One Person

You forego time with your friends and family to be with this other individual. You prioritize them above all else, and you never want to imply that you cannot be by their side. Holiday meals at your parents' place may be shortened, and nights out with your friends may become scarce as you devote all of your time to this one individual.

#9. Demonstrating the Halo Effect

To you, anything and everything this person does is amazing. Additionally, whatever you do for them must be flawless. You may own an item of their clothes that you constantly sleep in or a photograph near your bed that you frequently stare at until you fall asleep.

Why do individuals exhibit these symptoms? And how do people become obsessed to the point that their entire universe revolves around someone else? Consider a few possible explanations for this.

Why do we obsess over someone?

There has not yet been a definitive cause of obsessive love established. It is, nevertheless, frequently present in certain types of mental problems, such as borderline personality disorder (BPD). It is also possible to have it in those diagnosed with obsessive-compulsive disorders (OCD).

Individuals with BPD and OCD share underlying obsessional symptoms, and love is far from the only location where this condition might show. However, it is one aspect of a person's life that others may see, particularly the object of affection.

This kind of OCD consumes sufferers with concerns about their relationships. They doubt their lovers' love and attraction to them, their compatibility with them, and the extent to which their partners love them.

While having reservations or suspicions about a spouse is natural, persons with ROCD have illogical beliefs that are unjustified and destructive to their lives.

How to Stop Obsessing Over Someone in 9 Simple Steps

If your obsession with someone is wreaking chaos in your life, here are nine tried-and-true strategies to stop the unhealthy attraction.

1. Destroy Their Pedestal

When we're drawn to someone, it's easy to overlook their imperfections. Consciously highlighting their flaws can assist you in overcoming the addiction. Consider everything about this individual that you dislike or wouldn't want in a partner. Increase the prominence of these areas to demonstrate that there is a balance and that the individual is not perfect.

Additionally, consider the negative experiences you've had with this person. Consider the times you were freaked out by their actions or the night they walked out on you during a disagreement. These are the times when this individual reveals their true colors, so avoid focusing exclusively on the positive aspects of their past.

2. Refrain from Using Their Ideas to Determine Who You Are
When we're fascinated with someone, we generally hold their perspective in high regard, regardless of how ludicrous it may be. If this individual denigrates you with harmful comments, it's time for them to be removed from your life. You deserve affection and respect. You are not a victim of your history, and it has no power to define you unless and until you allow it to.

Allow no one to convince you that there is no possibility of positive change or growth in a new direction because there always is. Thus, you will experience a sense of confinement, limitation, and hopelessness. Anyone who wishes to keep you thinking in this manner is likely to do so out of discomfort with the positive changes occurring in your life and fear of losing you as you progress and move on to better things.

In your life, you must be the final decision-maker. You do what is best for you in the long run and ignore anyone who attempts to limit you or your potential.

3. Get a Support System
Enlist the assistance of your friends to assist you in coping with and overcoming an obsession. Your friends and family are almost certainly well aware of the situation, and they can provide you with that all-important viewpoint from the outside. Their perspective enables you to comprehend yourself and the other person. Perhaps you overlooked certain red flags or bad characteristics that they saw. If necessary, choose

an accountability partner to communicate with when you feel overwhelmed by obsessional feelings.

Additionally, they will be able to provide you with comfort and support throughout this time. When the opportunity presents itself, take it. Invite your buddies over for dinner or a drink. Avoid spending your days alone at home, drowning in your sorrows. Continue living your life since the other person is continuing to live theirs.

4. Accept That You Don't Need Them in Your Life

This may be the case with a new crush or an ex-partner. You may desire somebody, yet they bring nothing constructive to your life. Consider the possibility that you're better off without someone who doesn't value or cherish you. Consider that you should not have to persuade someone to stay or desire to be with you. Additionally, consider how successfully you lived your life before meeting this individual.

At first, it will be tough to identify that you no longer require this person in your life. However, in time, it will become increasingly clear. After some time, you will understand that you are in an ideal situation without them.

5. Develop a Mindfulness Practice

If you do nothing to interrupt your obsessive thought patterns, you will get caught in your compulsive behavior whenever you begin to think about this individual. Therefore, whenever you think of the person, come to a halt. Recognize when you've succumbed to an obsessive mental process. Once you can identify your ideas as they arise, you may begin to control them.

Mindfulness requires work, but once mastered, the rewards are numerous. You'll be able to rest your mind and body as a result. The practice of mindfulness has been around for a long time and has proven to be durable. Experiment with mindful meditation and be receptive to the idea that it can assist you in shifting your mentality.

6. Take a Step Back

Distancing yourself from the object of your fixation allows you to redirect your attention to your own life. This may entail temporarily relocating to another city or avoiding locations frequented by the other person. We are creatures of habit who follow a week-to-week schedule.

Habits and routines provide comfort and a sense of security. However, at this point, you're hoping to break free of that routine to stop obsessing. If you do things that remind you of this person, you're not attempting to remove them from your thoughts; rather, you're attempting to keep them in your life.

Now is the moment to establish new habits. By altering your behaviors, you instruct your brain to wake up and be present, which is exactly the type of brain pattern you require. And what if your levels of obsession are excessive? Then, you must seize control and proceed.

This will assist you in restarting your life in a new location. You will be prepared for the future rather than bound by the past. For those prone to obsessive behaviors, remaining in the same spot for an extended period can significantly increase emotions of repetition. Your environment affects your perspective and thought patterns.

7. Trace the Source of Your Obsession

This may entail digging deep within and inquiring about your relationship with your primary providers. It will almost certainly cast light on why you're currently enamored by someone and why you seek a connection with someone emotionally unavailable.

Investigate attachment styles and attempt to determine which one you possess. This may explain your relationship behavior and your need to cling to individuals even when they don't reciprocate your feelings.

8. Find Something New to Do

Commit to expanding your knowledge in the following weeks. It teaches you new skills and gives you something else to focus on besides the person you're obsessing over. Perhaps discovering new hobbies appears to be a generic answer to many of life's difficulties, but that's simply because it's extremely successful. Acquiring a new talent can rewire your brain and alter your perspective, allowing you to break free from your obsessive cycle. For instance, if the subject of your infatuation has always shown a dislike for museums and documentaries, now is the moment to indulge in these activities that you have been forced to forego previously for that person's sake. Alternatively, if you're passionate about a certain subject, invest in educational materials and establish yourself as an expert.

9. Seek Expert Assistance

If your obsession with someone is impairing your entire quality of life, you should visit a health practitioner to assess whether medical assistance is warranted. Even though talking to friends and family can be highly therapeutic, it's not always the greatest option for people with severe obsessive thoughts.

Speaking with a specialist can assist you in determining what is driving you to think about this other person, what aspect of them is resonating with you, and how you can begin shifting your thought patterns. You'll identify your triggers and gain knowledge about redirection. A professional can assist you in navigating the path to recovery. Foster no resentment toward yourself for seeking professional assistance.

Final Thoughts on Someone You're Obsessed With We've learned that unrequited love can induce obsessions. A variety of factors can trigger obsessive love. Still, the primary message from this section is that being in a relationship with someone who doesn't reciprocate your feelings is extremely unhealthy. I hope the tactics discussed have provided you with some ideas for quitting obsessing about someone and moving on with your life.

My-mindguide.com

HOW YOUR OBSESSION WITH PERFORMANCE ALTERS YOUR PERCEPTION OF SELF

We live in a performance-obsessed society. Competitions, awards, and rankings are an inevitable part of life for the young and elderly.

How we perform—in the classroom, at work, on the sports field, or even in life in general–affects how others see us and how we perceive ourselves. This impact can be so strong in some circumstances that we grow to view our performance as an integral part of who we are.

Research examines this potential affiliation with our ability to perform, and we propose that we recognize and better comprehend what we refer to as performance-based identities.

Why do we base our identity on performance?

A performance-based identity develops when an individual not only recognizes their ability to succeed (or, on the other extreme, their complete incompetence) in something but also feels fundamentally characterized by that degree of performance. If they cannot maintain the same level of performance for any reason, they may lose their sense of self (or a big chunk of it).

Simply put, they'd have difficulty answering the age-old question, "who am I?" This would then generate a slew of complex issues about their role in the world and their purpose and options in life.

While not everyone develops a performance-based identity, we are all prospects. This is the case because we all live in a society that places a high value on success. Beyond the world of employment and formal performance appraisals, this concern with performance is prevalent. It is ingrained in our culture.

According to a recent poll of over 80,000 people globally, over 65 percent of respondents believed that being extraordinarily successful or having others recognize their accomplishments was essential to them. This emphasis on performance is evident in various ways in daily life. For the most part, the most popular television shows are all about outdoing one's peers in a certain field. In politics, voters are increasingly drawn to candidates who successfully depict themselves as "winners," regardless of the degree to which data support their statements.

Not a New Phenomenon

While performance-based identity as a concept is novel, the phenomenon is not. Around a century ago, Max Weber, a renowned German sociologist, created the concept of the Protestant work ethic. He argued that capitalism's psychological fuel was this religiously entrenched desire to work hard. In the 1980s and 1990s, Stanford University psychologist Albert Bandura and colleagues conducted an extensive study on the origins and consequences of self-efficacy, or what many people refer to as confidence (much to Bandura's chagrin).

Recent research by another Stanford psychologist, Carol Dweck, has sparked widespread interest in "mindsets"—people's beliefs about the malleability of their skills and abilities. These concepts highlight the impact of performance on our self-perception and behavior.

Why It Matters

Generally, we view performance-based identities positively and as having beneficial outcomes. Consider boxer Muhammad Ali's iconic reputation and his famous "I am the greatest!" poem. Similarly, people generally appreciate— even envy—the extreme self-confidence displayed by the world's best CEOs, actors, and artists.

Indeed, it is likely that performance-based identities have many beneficial effects on people who possess them. Defining oneself as outstanding at anything boosts one's self-esteem and confidence. Additionally, such an identity is likely to offer protection during substandard performances or periods of failure. If you and others are aware that you are a high performer, instances of less-than-stellar performance will be dismissed as transient aberrations.

Performance-based identities are also likely to protect against the well-documented "impostor syndrome," in which individuals devalue the significance of their talents and abilities in their accomplishments, resulting in feelings of inadequacy and self-doubt.

Nonetheless, these identities have a shadowy aspect. A good performance-based identity may leave a person feeling invincible, overconfident, and complacent about practice and progress. Elite athletes frequently discuss avoiding building a performance-based persona for just this reason.

Additionally, issues might develop when individuals label themselves as great performers but are unsure of their identity. In certain settings, individuals may be offended by even the most constructive criticism of their performance, or they may avoid assisting (or even sabotaging) their colleagues out of fear of losing their position at the top of the hierarchy.

Finally, negative performance-based identities—in which individuals perceive themselves as terrible performers rather than top performers—are likely to have various negative consequences, including low self-esteem and habitual avoidance of complicated tasks.

Additional research is required to determine the influence of performance-based identities on our lives. Meanwhile, Aristotle's observation that "understanding oneself is the beginning of all wisdom" serves as a reminder to all of us how our sense of self may be affected by persistent pressures to excel.

Why Are We So Obsessed With Accumulating Wealth If Money Doesn't Buy Happiness?

Melissa Leong, the author of *Happy Go Money*, takes a sledgehammer to our money beliefs in an excerpt to help us uncover what genuinely makes us happy.

This is something you've probably thought about before. Every day, we make decisions based on the belief that happiness can be purchased and that having more money makes everything better. We accept the new work that requires an additional hour in traffic since it pays more. We shelled out more for a coat because it's designer. We purchased the larger house because it includes a yard for future children and a kitchen island described as "an entertainer's dream."

To be honest, when we see something we desire, such as a new pair of shoes or the latest gadget, we do experience joy; it activates a region of the brain called the nucleus accumbens, or the so-called "sex and money" region. It's triggered when humans receive a reward, whether it is drugs, money, or food. Then, when we purchase anything, our brains receive a delightful blast of dopamine.

That may sound seductive and delectable, but the ecstasy doesn't persist. Then, we simply require further "stuff." All of the nonsense we purchase loses its luster. When the novelty wears off, and the endorphin and dopamine rush is depleted, we're left with a hole and possibly remorse.

"How come I spent money on this?" we inquire. The answers we supply? Because I need it. Because I'm deserving of it. Because I'd had a difficult day. Because I'm devoid of willpower. Because it was on sale. Because it's become a habit. Because it was a spur-of-the-moment decision—a knee-jerk reaction. However, when it comes down to it? Because I desire happiness.

Thus, what do we truly require to be happy? Let us dissect and rebuild our opinions on the matter.

The Magic Number

A certain sum of money is required by every one of us to be content. But . . . how much?

For those of us on the brink of losing our homes, concerned about feeding our children, and cringing when the phone rings in anticipation of a debt collector's call, there's no doubt that more money will make us happy. However, before we can tie money to joy, the rest of us need to define what it means to be "happy."

Neuroeconomic scientists (those who investigate how we make economic decisions) divide happiness into two categories:

1. *Life Satisfaction* – An assessment of your overall well-being (the type of happiness you are content within life in general)

2 *Daily Mood Swings* – the joy, stress, despair, rage, and affection you experience from moment to moment – how you feel today, how you felt yesterday. (The kind of happiness to which the majority of us can connect—present-moment bliss.)

The wealthier people become, the more content they are with their lives—to a certain extent. Globally, persons in wealthier countries report higher levels of life satisfaction than those in poorer countries. (Rich countries are more likely to have a calm political climate with fewer tyrants, which is good for everyone's wellbeing.) However, a 2018 Purdue University study found a cap: $95,000 US (pre-tax, per single-family household). Having more money didn't imply that you were more content. According to several studies, the threshold for daily pleasure is between $60,000 and $75,000 per household. According to the 2018 study, life satisfaction and daily happiness actually fall slightly as income increases once these incomes are attained.

What the what?

Once our basic requirements are addressed, we're motivated by other impulses such as pursuing more financial possessions and comparing ourselves to others, which contribute to our unhappiness. Additionally, high incomes can result in high demands (more working hours, more stress, and less time for family and leisure).

However, this doesn't mean we should all aim for the "feel-good" financial sweet spot of $75,000 each year. The studies are based on averages, and each of us requires unique things to be happy. However, we all find satisfaction in certain simple things—kisses, laughter, and comradery.

Consider some of your happiest moments from the previous week. Were you able to spend it with others? Were you able to enjoy an activity, such as running or catching up with a friend? Would a wad of cash have enhanced those moments?

Most likely not. If you answered affirmatively to the latter question, how much additional happiness do you require? Continue reading.

Your magic number is probably wrong

Let's undertake a joint exercise. How content would you say you are on a size of one to ten? Consider how much money you currently have in the bank, and consider your present salary. How much additional money would you require to earn a perfect ten?

Michael Norton, a Harvard Business School professor and co-author of *Happy Money: The Science of Smarter Spending*, polled average-income earners and high-net-worth Britons (those with a net worth of greater than $1 million) and asked them those questions. "Everyone agreed on two to three times the amount of money," Norton explained. That's a problem because people who have $1 million often say, "If I had $3 million, I'd be a perfect ten." Except that those who possessed $3 million stated, 'If I possessed $9 million, I'd be a perfect ten.'

Happiness, in essence, is a sliding scale, how much this might annoy you. Whatever you have, you will always desire more, even if your fortune is in the millions. When you discover the gold at the end of the rainbow, the pot is simply too small, and you're back on the hunt for more rainbows.

It's almost as if it's a curse. Additionally, it takes the luster out of my boyhood fantasy of winning a million dollars in the lottery. That was my very first fantasy: to win the lottery and marry one of the New Kids on the Block (anyone but Danny). Every weekend, I'd dress up, and we'd dine at Red Lobster. (Today, this is still my notion of a hot date.)

However, contrary to popular belief, winning the lottery does not entitle you to a one-way trip to Euphoria Town. Consider this well-known 1978 study, in which researchers questioned two very different groups about their happiness: recent Illinois State Lottery winners who won between $50,000 and $1 million, and recent victims of horrific accidents who were either paraplegic or quadriplegic. They asked lottery winners and accident victims to rate their happiness at that point in their lives, their happiness before the life-altering incident, and their anticipated happiness in a few years. They questioned how enjoyable they found basic tasks (talking with a friend, watching TV, eating breakfast, buying clothes, getting a compliment, etc.).

Seriously? Who's happier, the wheelchair user or the Lamborghini driver? Yes, the lottery winners were in the moment happy. The winners expressed a greater sense of present happiness. However, persons with impairments placed a higher premium on future happiness. They also exhibited a greater appreciation for the ordinary pleasures of life, such as hearing a joke or reading a magazine. Indeed, research indicates a relationship between great money and a diminished capacity for modest pleasures. Experts attribute it to hedonic adaptation—our propensity to become accustomed to whatever we have. Even a significant improvement in one's life eventually becomes the new normal. You don't smell the roses because they're present throughout the day. And research indicates that our internal thermostats are set somewhere between happiness and sadness: they fluctuate in response to circumstances but generally revert to the standard-setting. Thus, if you were a miserable moaner before winning the lottery, you will very certainly remain a wretched rich moaner.

In another genuine model, Markus Persson, the maker of *Minecraft* who offered it to Microsoft for $2.5 billion in 2014, apparently bought a $70-million manor complete with a treats divider, vodka and tequila bars, fashioner fire dousers (since security starts things out), and fifteen washrooms furnished with $5,000 controller-worked latrines with air deodorizers and warmed seats. However, he tweeted in 2015, "I'm hanging out in Ibiza with a group of buddies and partying with celebrities, able to do whatever I want, and I've never felt more alienated . . . The trouble with obtaining everything is that you run out of reasons to continue trying, and human interaction becomes impossible as a result of imbalance," he added in another tweet.

This could be distressing for you. It's *reassuring* to me. It teaches me that no single event, material possession, or external element defines my pleasure in the end. Adaptability is a characteristic of human beings. A million bucks or a disaster can become the new normal over time. While having money allows you to enjoy tastefully fighting fire with your Louis Vuitton extinguisher, it may also make previous pleasures appear less pleasurable.

Therefore, keep in mind that there are other ways to spend your money than playing the lotto. The chances of winning the Powerball big stake are 1 out of 292 million—and the chances are that having more cash won't forever make your days more joyful.

Your Happy Money To-Do List

- If you find yourself thinking, "If I only had (insert the desired item), I would be happy," challenge that thought. Request that your partner, coworker, or friend gently poke you if they ever overhear you repeat that sentence. It'll be similar to that dreadful baby shower game in which you are forbidden to mention "baby"—but for the rest of your life.

- Relying on anything (or anyone) else to make you happy is a waste of time and energy. If affirmations are your thing, jot down the following and post it somewhere: "I'm in control of my happiness."

- Identify three significant things that make bring you joy regardless of your financial situation (e.g., good health or a loving partner). Now, identify three extremely specific items (e.g., sleeping in on the weekend, your jam on repeat, etc.).

Repeat the practice whenever you're feeling down about your financial condition—or any scenario, for that matter.

- Put an end to your lotto playing. Now. Next time you're tempted to play the lottery, consider buying someone a cup of coffee or putting money in a donation box instead—for a guaranteed source of enjoyment.

Our Culture Is Obsessed With Sex For 5 Reasons

Western civilization is sex-obsessed. Sex is prevalent in our films, music, television, advertising, discussions, and social media, among other places. However, many individuals fail to ask why.

There are a plethora of possible explanations for this. Certain reasons are unquestionably more significant than others. And they almost certainly overlap. Nonetheless, the following five factors explain why western civilization is obsessed with sex:

Reason 1: Our culture has squandered its faith in God. Nietzsche declared over a century ago that God was dead and that we had murdered him. Of course, he didn't mean that humanity killed God, but the Western culture had abandoned God's concept. Even while many people pretend to believe in God today, as Nietzsche warned, our civilization has become effectively secular. And, in the absence of God, life lacks objective significance. It's pointless. As Bertrand Russell observed, we must construct our lives on "the immovable basis of despair." Since God and religion are no longer sources of transcendence, many people turn to sex for transient pleasure and purpose.

Reason #2: Our culture has eschewed the concept of immortality. Assuming there is no eternal life, the current second becomes basic. If death is imminent and there is no possibility of prolonged life, why not savor every moment of pleasure? If there is no resurrection, the Apostle Paul stated, "Let us eat and drink, for tomorrow we die" (1 Cor. 15:32). Depeche Mode recorded a song titled "Fly on the Windscreen" in the 1980s. The song's words describe how humans, like flies on a car's windscreen or lambs being led to the slaughter, are waiting to die. The song proclaims that death is imminent. Therefore, what should we do? "Come hear, contact me, kiss me, contact me now . . ."

Reason #3: Our culture has abandoned its belief in sex's sacredness. The sexual revolution's motto is that sex is trivial. Indeed, this narrative portrays sex as a simple physical action devoid of any spiritual dimension that many individuals engage in for recreational purposes. Liberation is great, but we should still view sex as a divine gift to be experienced within prescribed parameters.

Reason #4: Our culture doesn't believe that humans were made in the image of a creator. People who believe in naturalistic evolution think that humans came into being through a process that was completely blind, material, and without any thought or plan behind it. The same process that led to animals led to us. As a result, humans and other animals are only different in terms of their evolutionary status. If this were true, why wouldn't humans act like the rest of the animal kingdom? It makes no sense for us to act differently from animals because we're all alike. According to Nancy Pearcey, in her book *Saving*

Leonardo, Scarlett Johansson was asked about rumors that she has a lot of sex with other people. She said, "Yes, I do think that on a very basic level, we are animals, and by instinct, we kind of breed in the way that makes sense."

Reason #5: Our culture isn't very interesting. It's because Generation Z was raised in a culture where they can have anything and everything they want at any time, where they want, and how they want. There are a ton of TV channels, streaming music services, video games, and social media platforms that keep you connected and entertained all the time. Yet, the truth is that people are lonelier than ever. When we don't have meaningful lives, we live through stars instead of living them ourselves. For a culture that doesn't have a lot of meaningful relationships or a bigger goal in life, sex naturally becomes a big deal.

The Darwinian response is that if our forefathers hadn't been fascinated with sex, we wouldn't be here—which is reductive but unassailable. And then there is the Romantic response—which, while elevating, provides plenty of room for debate. Rather than stripping sex of its wonder and risking boredom, I'll follow the latter course and risk your disagreement.

Sex is enigmatic, frequently sublimely so. Sex can expose us to mockery or enlightenment. Nothing is certain about sex, except that it is consequential. According to philosopher Arthur Schopenhauer, the ultimate goal of all romantic relationships is more essential than all other goals in life. What it determines is the composition of the next generation.

Schopenhauer, who lived a century before the genome's decoding, wasn't referring to the genome's composition. Nor was he just referring to sex's demographic repercussions. He recognized that sexual love transcends gene exchange and reproduction; that our loves and their sexual consummation affect the makeup of our psyches and identities. Having sex is a conceptual wild card. If you want to be more creative, it is a necessary undertaking.

I discovered the Schopenhauer statement in a biography of Erwin Schrödinger, one of the founders of quantum theory and a notorious womanizer. Walter Moore explores new ground in his biography, *Schrödinger: Life and Thought*, by writing about his subject's love and scientific lives. He says that Schrödinger came up with quantum theory while living in a Swiss hut with a lover. What makes this noteworthy is that when asked to write about his creative life, Schrödinger declined, claiming that the role of his lovers was critical and that discretion would oblige him to leave it out.

Sex can transform hearts and minds in ways that nothing else can. It introduces us to our partners and teaches us about their beliefs, rhythms, and perspectives. A nobody can become somebody or vice versa under the hex of sex. Our regular perspective on the world is suspended temporarily, as is the script we follow. We see differently in the space created by sex and may recognize something we've neglected or notice something entirely new. That is what happened to Schrödinger. While the snow accumulated around his Alpine love nest, he was delving into the subatomic world's mysteries.

Of course, not every lover leads us to life-changing (or world-changing) revelations. Certain real or potential partners are personal poison, and it's critical to develop the ability to recognize them before jumping into bed with them. However, by focusing exclusively on seduction and mechanics, we risk losing sight of sex's unmatched capacity for transformation.

Even if there is no danger of unintended pregnancy or sexually transmitted illnesses, there is a need to exercise caution regarding who we sleep with. As eating affects our bodies' composition and well-being, sex affects the composition and integrity of our essential selves. Is it any surprise that we're so captivated by it? This honey is extremely sticky for a reason.

If anyone knows where the source is, please let me know. Still, I've heard Sigmund Freud quoted as claiming that sexual and intellectual investigation are mutually exclusive. D. H. Lawrence argued that "the intellect that emerges from sex and beauty is intuition."

Obsession
My-mindguide.com

HYPNOSIS FOR OBSESSIVE OR INTRUSIVE THOUGHTS

Do you feel as if your mind is a broken CD that is perpetually caught in the same old rut repeating the same old thoughts? Do these thoughts appear to barge in and remain, interfering with your life and putting you in a poor mood, frequently depicting the worst-case scenario, coupled with all the possible outcomes? This type of thinking can leave an individual feeling nervous, stressed, and tired. **Are you fed up with being the target of these unwanted thoughts?**

Break Free From The Cycle Of Obsessive Thoughts and Take Control Of Your Thoughts

How many have gym memberships, recognizing the critical nature of exercising our bodies and flexing our muscles?

However, how frequently can you say you flex your mental muscles by focusing on empowering and motivational thoughts? How often do you aim to empower and uplift yourself?

Too frequently, we neglect our mental workouts, and as a result, our minds and emotions can become overgrown and unruly with intrusive or compulsive thoughts. Having these thoughts flow in and out of our brains may frequently weaken us, erode our confidence, and be quite frustrating when there is no apparent remedy.

According to research, we may learn to manage and regulate obsessive or intrusive thoughts and rewire our brains to have a more optimistic mindset. And we may accomplish all of this by utilizing the mind's power.

The Six Crucial Steps to Breaking the Cycle of Obsessive Thoughts and Taking Control of Your Thoughts

Read on to discover six secrets to breaking the cycle of obsessive thinking and regaining control of your mind. This is accomplished through hypnosis, personal development counseling, and neurolinguistic programming. It has been demonstrated via his studies that those diagnosed with obsessive-compulsive disorder *do* have the potential to overcome obsessive or intrusive thoughts and rewire our brains using the power of the mind.

Step 1: Create new and positive thoughts

This is the stage at which we construct a new map or template for the positive thoughts and behaviors you wish to emphasize. These are healthy, empowering attitudes and behaviors that will help you develop self-confidence and self-esteem.

Step 2: Determine what causes the obsessive thoughts

Hypnosis can be used to discover the source of your intrusive or obsessive thoughts, as well as the reason(s) behind them. The hypnotist will be looking for the purpose behind your thoughts and any internal conflicts that may contribute to obsessive or intrusive thinking. Finally, any limiting ideas you may have about the world around you and your ability to cope with life will be examined. Once you've made these findings, you've already won half the battle because you'll fully grasp the unconscious drivers of your obsessive or intrusive thoughts.

However, knowledge alone is insufficient. To effectively manage our ideas, we must next develop and adopt new tools and techniques. These techniques and tactics will assist you in replacing unproductive ideas with proactive and beneficial thoughts and behaviors that will enable you to meet your emotional requirements healthily. Additionally, you will learn to deal with any unforeseen problems that arise in life in these fresh and constructive ways, rather than becoming trapped in a downward spiral of unproductive thinking.

Step 3: Incorporate innovative and resourceful strategies and tools for proactive thoughts and behaviors

This is the process by which customized techniques and coping mechanisms are developed for you—tools that will enable you to maintain an optimal state of mind and emotional resourcefulness in any situation. These skills include coping well with stress and processing and healthily transforming your emotions. Additionally, your subconscious inner capacity for dealing with and managing stressful situations will be studied.

Step 4: Identify your triggers

Next, your thought process must be broken down, allowing the hypnotist to identify the triggers that create or bring on obsessive or intrusive thoughts using hypnotherapy. These include both emotional or internal triggers or "defeating ideas" that contribute to obsessive thinking and environmental triggers. This thought process manifests itself in the images you construct in your mind's eye, the self-talk you engage in, and the way all of this makes you feel, which ultimately brings you down and creates a debilitating state of mind. After recognizing your internal triggers, we'll work on translating them into positive self-talk, proactive habits, and behaviors that will help you build a stronger sense of self-esteem and empowerment.

Step 5: Develop self-awareness and learn to direct and intentionally use your thoughts to create a positive mindset

To achieve the optimal state of mind conducive to emotional empowerment and healthy cognition, we must cultivate self-awareness of our own thoughts. These are the thoughts that both empower and disable us.

We will give you the skills and activities necessary to help you apply this sense of awareness to your ideas, feelings, and current state of mind. It's possible to control and direct your thoughts with these skills, removing unwanted thoughts and replacing them with more positive ones so that you can begin to "live" in an optimistic mindset.

Step 6: Rewire your brain for success to break the cycle of obsessive or intrusive thoughts

Consider the brain as a CD that you may insert into your computer. The information required to complete the task has been burned onto the CD, and all that is required of the laser in the CD player is to follow the patterns etched into the CD.

Your brain is analogous to the compact disc. Over time, any concept, pattern, or behavior that we engage in becomes burned or encoded into our brain's neural circuitry. This is our brain's method of increasing our efficiency. Consider your first time learning to drive a car. You were so aware of your foot's position on the petal that you sat upright and remained watchful—aware of everything going on around you. And you couldn't possibly hold a conversation or drink your coffee while driving. These new skills became encoded into your brain through consistent driving and became second nature to you. This is how you can hold a conversation or lose yourself in your thoughts for minutes at a time without needing to focus on every part of your driving.

It can be soothing to know that productive and beneficial behaviors are readily accessible since they are hardwired into our brains. However, it has been demonstrated that the useless encoded information in our brains does not have to be permanent.

Brain plasticity research demonstrates that we can alter an ingrained behavior or pattern in our brains. This can be accomplished by first becoming aware of our thinking patterns, breaking those patterns via awareness, and redirecting our thoughts to the new and healthy thoughts and behaviors we have developed. We can successfully rewire our brains in this new way of being by repeating this procedure.

Hypnotherapy Can Assist You in Gaining Control Of Negative, Obsessive Thoughts

Typically, OCD begins with a sequence of annoying and intrusive thoughts or pictures. These can include worries about making mistakes, wishing to harm someone, disease, imagined hazards, contamination, a fear of losing control, a concern that God will punish you for not being flawless, and a dread of anything else that may cause you pain.

These ideas are triggered by certain triggers, such as an ache or pain that makes you feel you have cancer, even though you do not. The concept repeats itself in your mind until you see the doctor for confirmation that you are cancer-free.

Obsessive ideas have a way of infiltrating the mind, forcing you to get out of bed and check that all doors are closed, and the stove is correctly turned off.

The Connection Between Worry and Obsessive Thinking

Worry is apprehensive anticipation of a negative event. Over time, worry has aided people in focusing their attention on issues that can be resolved successfully. This is how worry assists us in overcoming the difficulties of daily life.

However, this natural process fails for some people, trapping their minds in an endless process of attempting to analyze everything, particularly problems with no obvious solution.

When worriers are unable to perceive a solution to a problem and are unwilling to accept the facts of the situation, this is referred to as an unhealthy concern. This form of worry, called obsessive thinking, accounts for a sizable portion of the OCD problem. "Obsessive thinking" refers to the inability to regain control of recurrent, upsetting ideas and pictures.

The Harm That Worry Can Cause

Unhealthy worry can amplify and prolong distressing emotions, resulting in anxiety and additional worry. Feeling like you've lost control, you may succumb to the temptation to continually wash your hands or arrange your home in precise lines or squares to counteract the obsessive thoughts.

This procedure can continue indefinitely until you are sure that you have done everything possible to eliminate the thoughts. Each time intrusive, distressing thoughts plague you, the compulsive acts have the potential to become rituals.

The process then spirals into an endless circle of obsessive thoughts and compulsive behaviors in search of relief, which is, at best, temporary.

Attempting to Halt the Thoughts

Controlling obsessive thoughts will be extremely challenging if you are predisposed to obsessive mind patterns. You may have attempted to drive thoughts from your head and succeeded—but only for a few minutes. Indeed, research indicates that the forcing technique virtually never works and may exacerbate obsessive thought habits, resulting in mood disorders, despair, and anxiety.

The mind is divided into the conscious and subconscious minds, which has a considerable impact on the conscious mind. The subconscious mind's troubling thoughts flood the conscious mind, influencing your behaviors.

The issue is that you and your conscious mind are unsure about proceeding with these thoughts. Only a fully developed mind and a new perspective will enable you to overcome the obstacle.

How Hypnotherapy Can Assist You

- Hypnosis allows the therapist access to the subconscious mind, allowing them to clean out obsessive thoughts.

- Hypnotherapy works by helping you change your subconscious mind's negative mindset and replace it with positive recommendations from the therapist.

- A professional therapist will first explore to determine the underlying cause of the problem and then work with you to fully modify your attitude and responses in situations that may provoke obsessive thoughts.

Hypnotherapy is a fast-acting technique that is highly recommended for OCD disorders. It may be a long-term cure for obsessive thoughts that threaten to take over your life.

Can Hypnosis Truly Assist in the Treatment of Obsessive-Compulsive Disorder – OCD?

Around 4.3 million people of all ages in the United States are affected by obsessive-compulsive disorder (OCD). If the illness is severe enough, it can render some people helpless, preventing them from leading comfortable and productive lives.

It is typically treated with medication and/or cognitive-behavioral therapy (CBT), and other complementary and alternative therapies, including hypnosis. I'll explore each of these in further detail in this section.

At the moment, there are no medical tests available to identify the illness; instead, it is determined by a physician's assessment of the patient's symptoms and behaviors and the impact on the patient.

As with many other mental health illnesses these days, the professional agreement is that biological and environmental variables most likely contribute to the Disorder or put a person at risk of developing it. There's some evidence to suggest it runs in families.

While OCD cannot be prevented, early diagnosis and treatment can bring relief from symptoms and the potential for a near-normal life for the majority of those affected.

Treatments for OCD:

There are several treatment options for OCD, including medication and behavioral therapies. When it comes to therapies, do your study and consult a specialist before going on a selected path, as certain therapies can appear intimidating.

When it comes to treating OCD, medication is typically the first line of defense. Doctors frequently prescribe antidepressants since they have found that they regularly assist in alleviating symptoms. The most commonly prescribed medications are "Prozac" and "Zoloft." However, there are others, and a doctor can monitor and administer alternative medications if the patient doesn't respond to the more commonly prescribed medications.

These medications are all classified as serotonin reuptake inhibitors (SRIs), which have been demonstrated to be the most effective in treating OCD.

Between 40 and 60 percent of OCD sufferers benefit from medication. However, as is customary, consult with professionals, understand the potential side effects, and of course, monitor. These are powerful medications, and their usage should not be taken lightly.

Psychotherapy, or talk therapy, in which the therapist assists the patient in gaining insight into their illness and effectively assists the patient in alleviating symptoms via their awareness of the triggers, has had minimal success in helping persons with OCD thus far. However, this is not to say it should not be tried initially; as with all therapies, the therapist's expertise and understanding play a role in its success.

Cognitive-behavioral therapy is a frequently used second line of defense (CBT). This can be used in place of or in addition to medications. One type of cognitive-behavioral therapy known as Exposure and Response Prevention (ERP) effectively treats OCD.

ERP therapy entails the patient purposefully exposing oneself to whatever triggers make them anxious to indulge in their obsessions under the supervision of a competent therapist.

The assumption is that "when you choose to tackle your fears and obsessions, you must also resolve to not succumb to compulsive behavior." When you abstain from obsessive habits, you will notice a gradual decrease in your anxiety level."

To be certain, initiating Exposure and Response Prevention therapy can be a challenging decision. It may appear as though you are deliberately putting yourself at risk. However, It is critical to understand that Exposure and Response Prevention affects both your OCD and your brain. You begin to question and realign your alarm system (your worry) with what is truly occurring.

One thing to keep in mind about talk therapies and CBT is that they are all focused on the conscious mind, which accounts for approximately 10 percent of the human mind while ignoring the triggering of ingrained obsessions and compulsions in the unconscious mind.

Thus, while drugs and ERP can alleviate symptoms for many patients with OCD, many still struggle and seek alternative treatments.

On the other hand, the alternatives are viewed as contentious by some physicians and therapists who rely only on drugs and cognitive behavioral therapy or are generally unable to assist beyond those treatments. These same individuals would rarely bring up other therapy. This, however, is a disservice to patients who are unable or afraid to undergo ERP therapy.

Your Inner Self: 4 Simple Steps to Meditation Awakening

On the inside, your inner self is who you truly are. To understand one's inner self, one must first understand one's purpose, values, vision, objectives, motivations, and beliefs—not what others have informed you but what you have learned on your own.

These ideals don't accurately reflect who you are on the inside. Understanding one's inner self takes much introspection, self-awareness, and inner self-meditation.

Inner Self Definition: The phrase "inner self" refers to the spirit (heart) and mind, as opposed to the "outer self," which refers to the physical body and social connections.

Do you lie awake at night or daydream about living in a world where issues don't exist for you in your daily life? Consider what life would be like if you had unlimited funds, the ideal partner, children, car, job, education, and body.

Wouldn't you like to wake up feeling unstoppable, in control, and never exhausted or stressed? Wouldn't it be wonderful if you could simply float through your day with all your wildest fantasies materializing right before your eyes? Hold on a minute, though. Is this even possible? The answer might surprise you . . .

Finding Your True Inner Self

When you commit to discovering your inner self's motivation and spiritual process, you will create a meaningful, loving, and peaceful life. (Remember that this is a cause-and-effect dimension.) In reality, the majority of people struggle with their inner selves or aren't even aware they exist.

However, after you grasp the ideas, you may be pleasantly shocked to discover that the ideal life you could ever envision is nothing like expected—and much better.

The critical process of developing an awareness of your inner self will result in a life worth living and bring harmony and balance to everything you do and create in the future.

If this is a goal for yourself, you have come to the perfect spot. There are few meditation techniques more critical than this one for yourself. Let's begin your path toward self-awareness on the inside.

1. Remind yourself who you are

According to metaphysics, everything that manifests in your life begins on the inside and then manifests in the external world of your experience. As is true within, so is true without. Thus, what is the issue with our lives? To be honest, nothing. The issue boils down to our expectations, such as the demand for more love from others around us.

One way to improve our lives is to list our most significant goals, beliefs, and core values that correspond with the life we desire. Seven basic qualities define life from the heart that, when exhibited in our daily lives, enable us to operate as a portal to our deepest self or soul energy: appreciation, compassion, forgiveness, humility, understanding, and valor. That is excellent, but what is the seventh value? All six values combine to form the ultimate value, Love.

This is the person we may become on the inside to manifest this soul energy and become attuned to the work we are doing on our inner self to live a life of serenity and true lasting joy.

2. Identify who you are today and begin the process of self-discovery

Conduct some research on these six values and consider your life thus far. Where have you excelled in these ideals, and where have you fallen short thus far in your life? This will enable you to comprehend how you might make a genuine attempt toward betterment and begin the process of living an actual life on the inside.

3. Recognize your next steps to establish a balance between your inner and your external worlds

Understanding these six values and how they apply to your life will enable you to identify the source of the imbalance. Be compassionate toward yourself, let go of the past, and begin anew today.

Remind yourself frequently to cultivate self-motivation and drive through calm reflection and profound meditation by following the six ideals. It is critical to find a method to spend each day in isolation and meditation if feasible. Meditation and seclusion will help relax your nervous system and cleanse your thoughts, allowing you to build the life you desire.

4. Energize your intuitive self-meditation, which produces results in the "real world"

By learning to meditate, you may clear your thoughts and focus on visualizing the world you desire to live in. This helps your inner self emerge into your life, allowing you to make critical life choices based on who you truly are, rather than what others or the media want you to be.

Take a moment to download a fifteen-minute meditation music mp3 or watch a meditation video below and visualize the life you truly desire by practicing the six heart virtues to the fullest extent possible.

Through Meditation, Discover Your True Self

Life is a narrative that we create with the thoughts, sensations, and emotions we encounter in each instant. Nonetheless, we spend most of our lives dwelling on our recollections of the past and our expectations for the future. We rarely experience the purity of the present moment. These ingrained memories and future expectations that we carry with us contribute to the daily stress we experience. Indeed, the average human is a collection of conditioned reflexes and nerves constantly triggered by external stimuli. Frequently, the conditions are just the ups and downs of daily life. However, there are times throughout our life when the responsibilities, pressures, disappointments, and fears can feel overwhelming.

Some people find themselves in toxic relationships that end unexpectedly; others realize that long-term employment no longer nourishes them, and there are even seasons in our lives when imbalances in our health and well-being occur. We have frequently defined ourselves in terms of our roles in specific relationships or employment. “I am a mother,” “I am a wife,” “I am a manager,” “I am a vice president,” and so forth. When these roles and parts of our lives—which we have relied on for so long to define ourselves and provide us with self-esteem—cease to meet our requirements, we can experience a sense of loss, emptiness, or bewilderment.

Fortunately, there is an age-old method for reestablishing this connection to our inner self: meditation, which enables us to experience our source. We come to understand that we are not the patterns and eddies of desire and memory that flow and swirl in our consciousness due to this experience. Although these patterns of desire and memory are the medium through which we appear, we are not these swirling fluctuations of thinking. We are the thinker who thinks, the observer who observes, the flow of attention and awareness, and the boundless ocean of consciousness. We spontaneously recognize that we have options and may exercise them naturally, not via willpower alone. We progressively restore peace, joy, and love to our souls through meditation and, in the process, rediscover our unconditioned self, which can never truly be lost.

We can reclaim our connection to a calmer, more tranquil life by gently wiping away the stress, tension, fear, and bewilderment that frequently follow someone who is at a crossroads. We can enjoy a life of happiness, harmony, balance, and tranquility from that point forth.

When a Student Is Prepared

Over the years, I’ve frequently been approached by people who tell me that after developing a meditation practice that lasted weeks, months, or even years, they simply quit meditating for whatever reason. In some situations, their daily routines shifted, and they no longer felt the need for a ritual that connected them to stillness and silence. They began a new job in other instances and opted to devote their entire time and attention to it rather than their meditation practice.

Some have expressed frustration with the lack of improvement they were experiencing. Naturally, this is all part of the process of letting go of our ideas and concerns, which will eventually connect us to pure consciousness—the magnificent joy of the gap. However, some misunderstand restlessness as a hindrance rather than a beneficial aspect of the process without enough education.

Then some individuals have waited their entire lives to begin a meditation practice and are now ready to reduce stress, relieve anxiety, bring quiet to the chaos, feel peace of mind, and connect more deeply with their inner voice on the journey to higher levels of consciousness. "When the learner is ready, the instructor will emerge," according to an ancient Buddhist proverb. This is particularly evident with regard to meditation.

Whether you've 1) meditated and enjoyed it but haven't formed a regular practice; 2) taken a break from meditation and are ready to return, or 3) have never tapped into your inner stillness and silence, today can be the first step toward discovering your soul. Once you've caught a glimpse of your soul, everything else in life appears to glow with the brilliance of happiness.

How is meditation performed?

We are all engaged in a continuous mental dialogue in which the meaning and emotional associations of one thought trigger the next, most often without our awareness. Buddhist psychology refers to this process as samskara, which can be thought of as mental grooves that lead thoughts in a particular way. Our samskaras are formed from our memories and can repeatedly compel us to react in the same limited way. Most individuals construct their identity based on samskara without even understanding it.

We interrupt the unconscious development of ideas and emotions during meditation by concentrating our attention on a new object of attention, whether it is a mantra, our breath, or an image.

Stuck emotions can be released, and our true selves, which aren't limited by anger or fear, can be reconnected through meditation. Meditation returns us to the tranquility of present-moment awareness. It provides a sensation of profound relaxation that dispels weariness and long-standing stressors and—as countless studies have demonstrated— promotes bodily and mental healing. Meditation benefits include the following:

- decreased blood pressure and hypertension
- decreased heart rate
- decreased cholesterol levels
- decreased production of "stress hormones" such as cortisol and adrenaline
- increased oxygen utilization by the body
- increased production of the anti-aging hormone DHEA
- improved immune function

Apart from these considerable health benefits, meditation's greatest gift is the sense of serenity and inner peace it instills in our daily lives. When we meditate, we transcend the mind's noisy chatter and enter a different realm: the silence of an unencumbered mind.

With consistent practice, the wide consciousness you enter during meditation begins to permeate your life outside of meditation sessions. You may experience brief bursts of joy and notice emotions of well-being wash over you periodically. You will notice an increase in your buoyancy and a sense of love and calm in your heart. Your thoughts, actions, and reactions are imbued with an extra dose of compassion and mindful awareness. All of these are indications that you are living in harmony with your genuine spiritual self, which results in a greater appreciation and knowledge of existence's divine quality.

In 4 Simple Steps, Discover Your Inner Self

I've stayed awake for hours many a night, thinking about what my life would be like if all my worries vanished. If I had no debt, had access to all the schooling I could ever want or need, a fully updated wardrobe, and the perfect hair, body, and smile, my life would be so much easier. I could wake up every morning feeling invincible and never have to deal with fatigue or stress. It would be ideal . . . or *would* it?

Many people struggle with discovering their inner selves. Once discovered, it has the potential to transform your life into the best it has ever been. The significance of knowing your inner self is that it helps you maintain balance and calm in your daily life. Who wouldn't desire such a thing?

1. Recall your identity

The first step in understanding what makes you unique is to examine who you are on the inside, below the superficial projection. Allow yourself to be loved unconditionally and create a list of your values, ambitions, morals, and beliefs. The inner you comprises everything that makes you happy or miserable on the inside. Being in sync with your inner self is critical to happiness.

2. Determine your current location

Once you've compiled a comprehensive list, set it aside and create a short timeline of your life. Draw attention to the highs and lows, as well as pivotal points. Make a note on the side of any areas where you adhered to your list of principles and morals and those you did not. Additionally, you will be able to see exactly where you are sitting today.

3. Recognize your next steps

With your timeline, you can understand exactly what has to be done to reestablish equilibrium with your inner self. Restart with a blank slate. Changes might be as easy as purchasing more organic foods or as complex as changing careers. Develop your ability to rely on yourself. Regardless of how difficult or simple your next steps are, you may continually remind yourself by staying connected to your inner self and drawing strength from there through contemplation and meditation. Indulge in isolation.

4. Stimulate your mediation

When you meditate, you can empower yourself by emptying your thoughts and focusing solely on the fact that you are focusing on your inner self. Consider your life now and how it may be if you followed your inner self rather than your outer self, making choices based on who you are, not who you might become.

By energizing my meditation in this manner, I can lie in bed at night and visualize my life exactly as it is. I picture myself making choices based on who I am, and I can go off to sleep, never wanting more because I know there will never be another me.

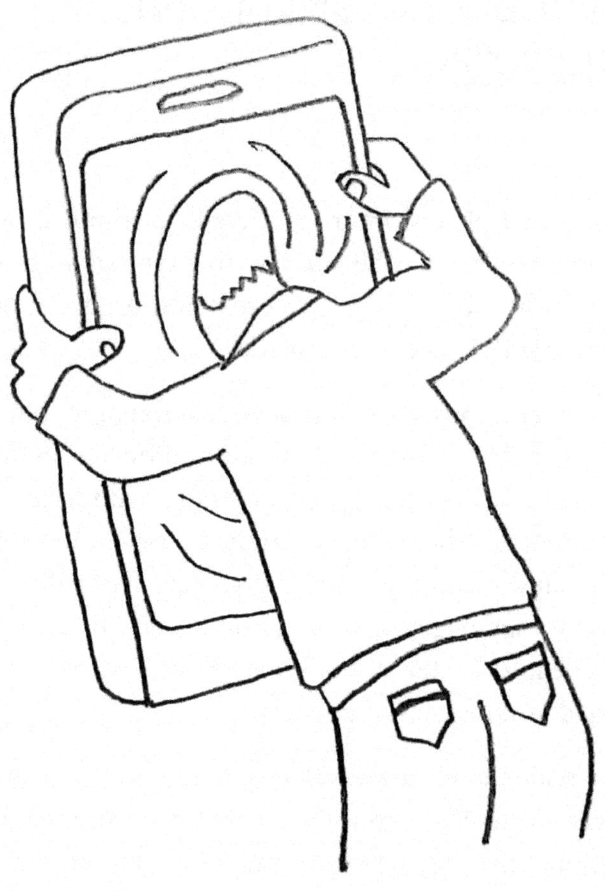

My-mindguide.com

WHAT IS THE DISTINCTION BETWEEN PASSION AND OBSESSION?

Passion and obsession are two states of mind in which an individual is intensely driven to exert significant effort. While passion motivates you to grow and progress, obsession has a detrimental effect on your life.

Passion and obsession are two overlapping but distinct realities. The first corresponds to an outpouring of emotional energy that causes one to push one's boundaries to their breaking point. The second paralyzes or limits will. Thus, obsession and passion are mutually exclusive truths. In other words, you may begin something out of enthusiasm and then cross a line into the territory of obsession. Thus, obsession may be defined as an excess of passion.

It is realistic to assert that passion and obsession are opposites. Both of these subjective realities require a high level of emotional involvement and undivided attention and focus. However, one embodies the constructive aspect, while the other embodies the destructive.

Obsession and Passion

Often, passion and obsession follow a path defined by external causes. It usually begins with an activity you enjoy and discover an unexpected source of joy. The work is so captivating that an individual develops a passion for it. Passion motivates you to devote a significant amount of time to such a task and attempt to improve it by raising the bar for demand and perfection. Then comes accomplishment and, with it, acknowledgment for such an endeavor, which is when the difficulties may arise.

External approbation, it turns out, can be detrimental. What was once spontaneous and enjoyable has become a means of obtaining positive reinforcement from others. You no longer take pleasure in the process but solely in the outcome. As a result, you develop an obsession with it.

The Labyrinth of Obsession

When you develop an obsession with a certain activity due to the response you receive from the results, joy transforms into worry. You develop an increased reliance on others and experience restlessness and stress. Indeed, some research indicates that this reliance may even result in immoral actions.

As a result, the need for external validation spirals out of control and develops into an obsessive passion characterized by restlessness and even frustration. This is not only an emotional but also a bodily reliance.

Evidence shows that a preoccupation with external acceptance floods the body with dopamine and develops into an addiction. This, of course, strengthens the reliance, and a person begins to view the world through a completely new lens. There is effort, even tiredness, and an element of uncertainty all simultaneously. They may even feel compelled to deceive to obtain approval.

Reliance on External Approval

Very few people are capable of entirely distancing themselves from the opinions of others and reaching a point where their approval is irrelevant. It requires a highly evolved individual to accomplish as much. Thus, simple people rely on the approval of others.

After all, who doesn't enjoy receiving an award or credit for their efforts? For example, most people experience some level of gratification when they publish something on social media and receive a "like," when they receive a friend request, or when their following grows.

The key to avoiding slipping into the traps of a fixation with other people's praise is to be aware of it. You must recognize that when you obtain a "like" for an unpretentious statement you made, what matters most is that you voiced it and that others found it thoughtful. The remainder is a bonus. It may be present today, but it may not be tomorrow.

There is much to gain from appreciating what you do and from being consistent with your thoughts without feeling stressed about the outcome. It is not simple to overcome the motivation that others' responses imply, but you must strive at it. Always strive to avoid falling into that trap. Thus, allow your passion to guide you, not your obsession.

Recognize the Distinction Between Passion and Obsession

You might be passionate about a variety of things that offer you joy and increase your energy level, but an obsession consumes your life and depletes your energy. You might be passionate about diet, yoga, or guitar playing. You can become fixated with *Instagram*, money, or current events.

Naturally, the things I described earlier that you could be passionate about can also become obsessions. A fine line is often encountered, and it's difficult to determine when something will cease to be delightful and become distressing. When anything begins to restrict your life or causes you to disregard tasks that you should be performing, you have entered obsessive territory.

Being enthusiastic about something improves mental health and provides a sense of purpose and fulfillment in life. Passion and obsession are inextricably linked in the Taoist tradition. Whereas passion is a constructive preoccupation, obsession is a destructive passion. It boils down to whether your concentration is on something that makes you feel better and more energized or on something that makes you feel worse and depleted of energy.

All of your thoughts will be consumed by an obsession. It will develop into a psychological addiction. Something your ego will be powerless to overcome. You feel compelled to pursue whatever obsession you have, even if it makes no objective sense in reality. It may fill your thoughts and be all you want to do from the moment you get up until the moment you go to bed, or you may pass out while obsessively performing it.

How to Put an End to Obsession

There are several strategies for escaping the obsessive hole. You can experiment with each to determine which ones work best for you. The first step toward overcoming an obsession is acknowledging that you have one. Determine the exact focus on which you are fixated. Following that, perform one of the following:

Relax

- Put on your headphones and lie down to listen to music.
- Submerge yourself in a sensory deprivation float tank.
- Step outside and take a walk around the forest.
- Breathe deeply with pranayama.
- Engage in attentive meditation.
- Submerge yourself in a hyperbaric chamber.
- Tone your body.
- Schedule a massage.

These eight ways of minimizing obsessive thoughts will be extremely beneficial to you—some more so than others. One of these options may be more aligned with what works for you to overcome an obsession. All of these will help you calm your thoughts and temporarily put your ego on hold. A relaxed body is conducive to a peaceful mind. While some of them may be unfamiliar to you or appear unusual, they have proven effective in reducing obsessive thinking in others and can do so for you as well. Allow yourself to unwind. Often, the greatest impediment to happiness and relaxation is our thinking. Turn it off for a bit and revert to a state of mind that benefits rather than exhausts you.

It's easy to confuse the two because passion and obsession are so similar. However, most of us believe that enthusiasm is more positive than an obsession. Because everything is energy, we can tell the difference by sensing something's energy. Is it energizing or draining us? Obsessions might deceive you into feeling more energized when, in fact, the energy has a fierce character.

When you direct all of your focus toward something, notice if you feel expansive and liberated or contracted and worried. This will indicate whether you are in a state of passion or obsession. If you're experiencing compulsive behavior, try one of the practices mentioned above.

When a Feeling Develops into an Obsession

It's wonderful to be passionate about our endeavors, whether they're work-related, sports-related, or involve other hobbies and interests. To be sure, this is frequently the case, but not always. It is contingent upon how we pursue our passions. As Professor Robert Vallerand, a positive psychology expert, explains, it depends on whether our enthusiasm is harmonious or obsessive.

To begin, some context. Sometimes, let's take a minute and appreciate having a solid obligation to something, particularly our work. Our passion may energize us and provide us with direction. It enables us to accomplish our objectives by devoting time to something we appreciate. It can contribute favorably to our sense of identity, particularly when combined with a variety of other interesting pastimes and interests.

However, our passions tend to spiral out of control. Our relationships could be put at risk, and we could suffer from burnout if we are so pushed to work that our time at the office exceeds what is essential. Could it be that our sense of identity is so entwined with our ability to perform effectively at work and in athletic competition that we feel devalued as people when we are unable to do so? What if we are so compelled to engage in an activity, such as a computer game (or, for that matter, *Pokémon Go*), that we neglect to do other critical chores and fulfill numerous responsibilities? Or perhaps we're so frustrated when we're forced to stop playing a game or pastime that we feel unfulfilled.

These are only a few characteristics of obsessive passion. It's similar to an addiction. Our approach is somewhat stiff or compulsive. We are compelled to continue with the action rather than selecting it freely. It's not as fluidly or harmoniously integrated into our other hobbies and interests. It may cause friction in our relationships. In competitive sports, obsessive passion may manifest as an excessive focus on winning at the expense of having fun with others and improving our talents. By playing with minor injuries, we may develop chronic ones. Otherwise, we may disregard warning indications related to our health or safety.

Engaging in harmonious passion is quite beneficial to our well-being. Regardless of whether it is a job or leisure, the action is consistently entertaining. It has a negligible impact on our relationships or other tasks. We can easily disengage from an activity consistent with our general lifestyle. It is by our principles. When we engage in an activity, we are often in a state of flow rather than feeling compelled to continue.

How are we following our many interests? Are those activities flexible and harmonious, or do they have a strict and compulsive quality? In either case, we will very certainly develop talents. Additionally, we are more likely to accomplish long-term goals when we are passionate about our endeavors in addition to being talented. However, whether our passion is harmonious or obsessive makes a significant difference to our well-being.

When Does What You Love Become Excessive Due to Passion And Obsession?

Are you someone with a deep passion? Is there something you adore doing so much that you feel excited simply thinking about it? Passion is an aspect of human existence that is arguably vital for survival. This is because if you are not enthusiastic about something in life, it is likely that you aren't content with your life—and there's a reason for this! Being absorbed in an activity or a task can be therapeutic and boost your sense of well-being, among other benefits.

You may be wondering if passion has anything to do with the brain. I'm pleased you inquired! Positive psychology is a relatively new branch of psychology. This is the psychology of positivity related to the impact of positivity on the brain and our behavior. This includes positive thinking, mindfulness, being grateful for what we have, and anything else that makes you feel good. While this may appear illogical and unsupported by science, there is substantial evidence that altering your cognitive processes can result in actual changes in your disposition and behavior.

According to Robert Vallerand's 2008 paper, *On the Psychology of Passion: In Search of What Makes People's Lives Worth Living*, we do things, particularly ones we are passionate about, to satisfy basic psychological needs. These are the autonomy, competence, and relatedness requirements. Isn't this logical, at least in some sense? As a species, we need to feel in control of our lives, efficiently interact with our circumstances, and be linked to other people.

These three guiding principles truly reflect who we are as a people. When you consider everything you do in life and why you do it, it frequently comes down to one of these three factors. We often love doing things that we excel at. Thus, when we excel at anything, we feel we have a greater sense of control over our lives.

Returning to Vallerand's investigation, he discovers two distinct types of passion: harmonious passion and obsessive passion. Obsessive passion occurs when you become so absorbed in an activity that you are passionate about that you subconsciously incorporate it into your identity. Typically, this control is imposed due to social or other pressures that virtually push you to continue with the behavior. Do you know how people have irrational health obsessions? Even if the health benefits are excellent, an individual is still engaged in the obsessive passion since their entire life gets consumed by eating excessively healthy food, going to the gym, and spending most of their free time discussing or thinking about healthy eating and exercise.

By contrast, harmonious passion occurs when you autonomously absorb something onto your identity. The distinction is that with harmonious passion, you are aware that you can choose whether or not to join in the activity and whether or not to incorporate it into your daily life. Rather than consuming the entirety of a person's life, it can coexist and interact happily with all other areas of that person's existence. Thus, someone truly passionate about music production can continue to work, go to the grocery store, and spend time with family, but then return home and make music for a few hours. If it were an obsessive desire, the individual would frequently feel compelled to engage in music-making rather than other activities. When we become fascinated by something, it becomes impossible for that obsession to coexist harmoniously with any other area of our lives.

This study demonstrates that our passions and how we express them can directly affect our health. When we pursue a harmonious interest, it can benefit our health; it can be detrimental to our health when we pursue an obsessive passion. A person who enjoys running will not only benefit from the exercise's health benefits but will also have a stronger sense of well-being and autonomy as a result of participating in an activity they enjoy. However, someone infatuated with running will feel forced to run in hazardous conditions such as rain or snow. According to the study, when we are fascinated by something, we are more prone to participate in harmful activities to accomplish our obsession.

Our relationships are subject to the same type of interaction. Being harmoniously passionate about anything may be an extremely attractive characteristic to someone and can demonstrate to your lover that you have something worthwhile to do apart from them. Additionally, because it is harmonious, you are not forbidding your significant other to accomplish the task, thereby convincing them that they are vital to you. Obsession with something, on the other hand, might have a huge negative effect on their contentment with the connection, as you are choosing to engage in an activity rather than the relationship. Surprisingly, this is equally true if your obsession is with the other person. Obsessive enthusiasm for a significant other can make them feel suffocated and as if they lack control in their own lives, resulting in a considerable decrease in happiness. Not to mention how off-putting it can be to have someone think and talk about you in every other aspect of their life to the point where they cannot engage in those other things.

Ultimately, passion is what makes life worthwhile. It's something we value so highly that it becomes ingrained in our identity. According to self-determination theory, we strive for and choose activities that make us feel autonomous, competent, and connected to others. There are two kinds of energy: agreeable enthusiasm, which includes being energetic regarding something that interfaces amicably with any remaining parts of your life, and passionate energy, which happens when your energy outweighs different needs and now and again encroaches on different parts of your life. Harmonious passion may have incredible consequences on your life and truly give it meaning. However, although still offering to mean, obsessive passion wreaks havoc on the majority, if not all, other facets of your existence. Therefore, it's imperative that you find something you genuinely enjoy doing, something you excel at, and something that brings you closer to other people because that makes the daily challenges of life worthwhile.

Are You Overly Obsessed with Discovering Your Passion?

"Passion" has gotten a lot of bad press recently. There appears to be a great deal written on why passion is bad.

The issue for most individuals is that they assume passion is the driving force behind their actions when, in fact, passion is an effect. Cal Newport debunks the misconception that we should be looking for passion in his book, *So Good They Can't Ignore You: Why Skills Trump Passion in the Quest for Work You Love*. Instead, he contends that through the acquisition of uncommon and valuable abilities, one can achieve a life of passion.

When you are entirely focused on "discovering" your passion, you are just considering yourself. If you focused on gaining talents and abilities to assist others, you would have a very passionate and fulfilling existence.

According to Jerome Bruner, a Harvard psychologist, "You are more likely to act yourself into feeling than you are to feel yourself into doing."

And this brings up a very critical aspect about passion that is rarely explored. There are two kinds of passion—one that you should pursue and one that you should avoid. The type of passion that most people desire is the type of passion that will destroy their lives.

Obsessive and harmonious passions are the two types.

Obsessive passion is defined as being entirely motivated and powered by emotion. It is really impulsive. This is the kind of passion in which you are unsure of your "WHY." In reality, you're looking for dopamine, self-esteem, or social acceptability, among other things. While excessive passion may appear and feel good at the moment, it always results in a messed-up life. Obsessive passion is defined as an activity that interferes with other aspects of your life and frequently results in addiction.

With obsessive passion, your emotions take over—another way of stating that your body has taken over your head and is craving dopamine.

On the other hand, harmonious passion is intuitive and naturally motivated and hence under your control. It is a result of deliberate intention and goal-directed activity. Harmonious passion improves all aspects of your life, ultimately making you a better person. According to the study, harmonious passion is significantly more associated with being in a flow state than obsessive passion.

Obsessive passion occurs when the subconscious mind seizes control of the conscious mind, leaving you feeling helpless. The driver has suppressed emotions and unresolved emotional conflict.

Harmonious passion is the deliberate rerouting and shaping of one's subconscious. Your habits and goals serve as the catalyst, and you continue to experience emotionally healthier and more balanced outcomes.

Why are people so perplexed by passion?

The world and the media promote intense enthusiasm as a desirable trait. It's seductive, extreme, artistic, and entirely driven by emotion. It's rash and eager to burn all bridges—including the most vital ones—to obtain what it desires. It's unorganized and rarely concludes happily. Additionally, this form of desire must be discovered rather than designed and created.

The harmonious passion is distinct. Undoubtedly, bridges must be burned, pledges to greatness made, and risks taken to live this type of enthusiasm. However, not every bridge. Instead of being motivated by impulse, harmonious passion is motivated by faith, vision, and confidence.

Confidence is a synonym for self-esteem. And with obsessive desire, you gradually lose trust in yourself since your current feelings fully dictate your behavior. While these emotions are thrilling, they represent the body in an addicted and self-defeating condition (more on this in a second).

Both sorts of passion experience peaks and valleys. However, obsessive passion's lows stem from remorse and neglect. In contrast, harmonious passion's lows stem from doubting whether what you're doing is still the correct thing, as well as from the obstacles of failure and progress.

10 Questions to Determine if Your Passion is Harmonious

1. When you have free time, do you divert your attention, or do you devote it to your passion/purpose?
2. How do you feel on days when you haven't worked on "it"?
3. What have you recently given up to embrace this passion more fully?
4. When was the last time you failed?
5. How have you changed positively in the last year to live out this purpose more fully?
6. Does your outward reality correspond to your inner thoughts, feelings, and dreams?
7. Are you more concerned with your peers' opinions or those of your family and friends?
8. Are your relationships with significant persons in your life improving or deteriorating?

9. Do you get a good night's sleep, or do you obsess over what you should be doing differently?
10. Is your life improving or deteriorating?

Do you divert your attention or devote it to your passion/purpose when you have free time?

We must exercise caution not to spend all of our available time on things that are simply good, leaving little time for what is better or best.

—Oaks of Dallin

It isn't comforting to observe how most people spend their time, desperately attempting to divert their attention away from reality.

A physical addiction generally results in strong emotions. Every emotion results from chemical processes occurring in the brain and throughout the body. And the body might rapidly develop an aversion to these compounds.

For instance, if you check your phone frequently throughout the day without thinking or choosing, your body is in control of your mind. Your body is attempting to release dopamine, which biologically supports your addiction. Your hand instinctively grasps your phone and performs its remembered and ritualized actions, and your intellect must catch up.

After some time, you become aware of what you're doing and resume conscious behavior control—at least until the next instance of subconscious self-sabotage occurs.

When you have a healthy passion and a compelling purpose, on the other hand, you spend your free time contemplating what you desire. You don't divert your attention away from reality. You accept reality. You're significantly more aware of everything going on around you—particularly of individuals and their emotional states. Thus, as your harmonious passion grows, you become increasingly emotionally intelligent because, at its core, harmonious passion is about connecting with and assisting other people.

What do you do when you have five spare minutes?

When no one else is looking, you are who you are. How you spend your time is a direct representation of your inner compass. If low-level distractions consume your time and you are continually besieged with subconscious dopamine-seeking cycles, you lack clarity about what you desire.

The more you accept a life of genuine learning and change, the more efficient your time management will become.

The more adept you are at planning your day around the future you wish to create—and then carrying it out—the more motivation and passion you will have in your life. Additionally, increased confidence can be expected.

Is it difficult to function if you haven't worked on "it"?

If your passion is harmonious, you will only experience regret if you allow distractions to divert you from what you know you should be accomplishing.

You lacked foresight and prioritized incorrectly. As a result, you allowed life to happen and neglected to focus on your art.

With a harmonic passion, you will never regret spending time with your loved ones or engaging in other hobbies or interests. You are aware that your "passion" is heightened only when the rest of your life is stable. For instance, in the book *Creative Quest*, Questlove discusses the significance of branching out from one's primary focus.

On the other side, if you have an obsessive passion, you are willing to waste significant amounts of time on distraction and then delve headfirst into your passion in a fierce and impulsive state. You're fine with abandoning critical priorities and relationships since your life is a disaster. All that matters now is obtaining that dopamine surge. Obsessive passion is entirely focused on you. It's fully self-centered, and in the long term, it results in a brief creative life owing to escalating internal and external tensions.

What have you recently given up to completely embrace this? *How is success ultimately quantified?" It is not about how much time you spend doing what you love that matters to me. It is the amount of time you spend doing what you despise.*

—Neistat, Casey.

If you're not increasingly allocating your time to more beneficial pursuits, you haven't grown your interest fully.

When you discover something that truly matters to you, you'll make sacrifices to spend more time doing what you love.

Jim Collins states in his seminal book *Good To Great*, "If you have more than three priorities, you don't have any."

As the quality of your daily actions improves, you have a greater understanding of what matters most to you. Clarity is achieved by exemplary behavior. Clarity and harmonious emotion are inextricably linked.

You know what to do already. Step two is already on your radar. You're aware of the areas where you are currently working at substandard levels. You're aware that certain actions in your life are suboptimal.

Begin today by eliminating anything bad and refocusing your attention more clearly on what you already recognize as your primary priorities.

Concentrate on what motivates you. Concentrate on what speaks to you. It's acceptable if you don't have all of the answers at the moment. Take broad steps, and your vision will become clearer, your motivation and confidence will grow, and your passion will bloom. By removing things that are leading you astray, you can strengthen your harmonious passion.

When was the last time you were unsuccessful?
Unless you're willing to be incorrect, you'll never create anything truly unique. You cannot have passion if you are not actively engaged in learning. If you are not failing, you are not learning. Failure is an opportunity to learn. Clarity is achieved through feedback. Confidence comes from clarity. Confidence stems from self-trust. Confidence in oneself enables you to attempt things that are currently out of reach. Experimenting with things that are out of reach at the moment is how you evolve out of suppressed and subconscious routines.

Since last year, how have you made progress toward accomplishing this goal?
Anyone who isn't ashamed of who they were last year likely isn't learning enough.

If you're not evolving, you're not devoted to something worthwhile. Commitment necessitates change. If you're not compelled to change for something higher than yourself, you have no concept of what love is. You're still far too self-absorbed.

Self-obsessed individuals don't believe they need to change. They believe the world should self-organize around them.

Committed and passionate individuals are voracious learners. They minister to those closest to them and use their gifts to transform a certain set of individuals. They don't require willpower to perform their duties. They're being dragged ahead and are powerless to resist. They have attained self-actualization as a result of transcending themselves. Their lives are so full of meaning that they're frequently rendered speechless.

Without growth, there is no life. Humans were created with the ability to evolve and grow. Being trapped in a hidden cycle of unhealthy emotional addiction is *not* what you were created for. You were created to grow beyond your pain, to be healed of it, and then to help others with what you've learned.

How closely does your outward reality correspond to your internal thoughts, feelings, and dreams?

What is subconsciously imprinted is expressed. Matter and mind are intricately linked. When one is altered, the other is altered as well. Your environment is a mirror of how you feel about yourself.

How powerful is the environment in which you currently live? To what extent do your environment and the wider world inspire you?

Is your situation compelling you to reach greater heights?

Have you placed yourself in a position of humility and excitement? Did you realize that you can immediately alter your environment through powerful behavior and decision-making? Did you know that you can build an environment that always encourages you to perform at your best? Did you know that you may alter your appearance from the inside out and the outside in?

When it comes to making a shift, you have two choices. You can either operate independently of your current environment and emotions, or you can create an atmosphere that compels you to rise above them. *Both* are required.

You must constantly act, think, and live above your existing circumstances. Additionally, you must constantly surround yourself with people, projects, and obligations that humble you—compelling you to discover something within you that you were unaware existed.

Are you more concerned with the opinions of your peers or with those of your family and friends?

We spend money we don't have on things we don't need to impress people we don't like.

Who are you attempting to impress?

It doesn't matter how successful or confident you are; you should be able to relate to everybody. You can and should maintain a down-to-earth demeanor. This is how you attract even the world's most successful people.

Joe Polish, the creator of Genius Network, frequently criticizes people for their treatment of those "below them." Joe leads a high-level entrepreneurial mastermind group comprised of extremely successful individuals, observing the interactions between the geniuses and his team. Frequently, he observes these "successful" individuals neglecting and disrespecting his team members.

If you just show respect to others when you believe they can help you, you won't have many friends for long. According to Dan Sullivan, founder of Strategic Coach, it takes him less than ten minutes to determine whether someone's primary motivation is progress or greed. It's self-evident. You cannot fake genuineness. You cannot conceal that you are not truly listening and are only interested in speaking.

Regardless of your level of prosperity, you should constantly try to love and help those in need—the individuals you refer to as family and friends.

Are your connections with significant individuals in your life improving or deteriorating?

Wherever you are, ensure that you are present. If the most important relationships in your life are getting increasingly strained and complicated, you almost certainly have obsessive passion. You aren't prioritizing. You've become significantly out of alignment.

If you have a harmonious passion, your relationships with the important people in your life will improve due to your own growth.

As you grow as a person via your passions and holistic development, you'll develop a greater sense of responsibility for your family and friends. You'll become more generous and caring. You'll gain confidence and strength, and you'll inspire and assist them. You'll improve your listening skills. You'll be significantly more engaged as a result. You'll remain where you are because you'll be acquiring the ability to live in a flow state. The more harmonic and consistent your daily activities are, the more present-oriented you will be.

Are you able to sleep soundly at night, or do you spend your time contemplating what you should be doing differently?
Never sleep without first addressing your subconscious. A good night's sleep is a mirror of a clear mind. When you live an aware life, you will sleep soundly. Your sleep will be rejuvenating and refreshing. Your dreams will be vivid and vividly remembered. Because you've mastered the art of directing your subconscious mind while you sleep, it will constantly stretch and expand.

Sleep has the potential to be the most productive moment of the day for an individual. During this time, the brain performs some of its most creative and educational activities. However, if you cannot enter deep sleep and aren't utilizing your sleep for healing and learning, your days won't be as productive as they could be. You won't be able to study and grow at the same rate as children—a rate that should never cease.

Is your life improving or deteriorating?
Success isn't something to pursue; it's something to be drawn to by the person you become. Simply put, is your life improving or deteriorating? If the problem worsens over time, you either have an obsessive passion or your behavior is out of control.

When you have a harmonic passion, your life improves continuously. You improve. Your health improves. Your relationships improve. Your financial situation improves. Your atmosphere improves. Your life becomes increasingly focused on the things that truly matter. You understand that most things are irrelevant, and you have high enough standards to shun the majority of what the world has to offer.

Dr. Barry Schwartz authored an extraordinary book entitled *The Paradox of Choice: Why More Is Less*. Based on decades of decision-making study, Dr. Schwartz determined that the best decision-makers actively eliminate practically all alternatives from their lives.

The best selections are those that eliminate the greatest number of options. Similarly, Gary Keller's seminal book, *The One Thing*, invites us to consider the following: "What is the ONE thing that needs to happen today that will make everything else simpler or irrelevant?"

The majority of choices are poor ones. Having an excessive number of options results in decision fatigue or willpower depletion. Willpower is ineffective. Rather than relying on willpower, be deliberate. Make decisive choices that eliminate unnecessary options. Be self-assured enough to set fire to your boats. Maintain sincere commitments. Invest in yourself. Take a risk.

This is how you improve your life. You behave with intention. You take action. Your actions define who you are. What you repeatedly do defines you. You must make a decision.

The environment pressures you to relinquish your agency to emotional addictions such as dopamine reliance. Take control of your emotions. Take control of your life. Every day, improve it.

Live a life that is both harmonious and powerful.

Enhance Your Work Passion Without Becoming Obsessed

Work offers genuine joy to certain people. These individuals feel in control of their work, have a positive self-image when at work, and find their work compatible with their other pastimes. Psychologists define these individuals as possessing a balanced passion. However, another type of desire exists: namely, *obsessive passion*. Obsessively enthusiastic individuals experience an uncontrolled drive to engage in their work, experience more conflict between their passion and other parts of their lives, and their work contributes significantly to their frequently unstable and negative self-image.

According to some critics, obsessive passion can be advantageous during the early phases of a new venture, such as when starting a new business. I respectfully disagree. Rarely is obsessive passion beneficial. It is not only that persons with an obsessive level of passion are committed, focused, and dedicated. Obsessively passionate about their work, they are inflexibly, excessively, and compulsively committed, making disengagement impossible. As a result, individuals establish negative behaviors from the start, increasing the likelihood of burnout in the long term. Take note of the correlation between harmonious passion and flow—the mental state of being completely present and absorbed in a job. According to research, flow, not obsessive enthusiasm, promotes creativity. Positive emotions and intrinsic delight connected with harmonious passion, not the negative emotions, compulsions, and fragile ego associated with obsessive passion, propel one to greatness.

Every one of us has a small amount of obsessive and harmonic passion for our profession. The key to increasing your harmonious passion while decreasing your obsessive passion is to improve your harmonious passion while decreasing your obsessive passion.

How can we dial down obsessive passion and dial-up harmonic passion? Regrettably, little scientific research exists on the practical side of passion (a state of affairs I seriously lament). However, I can think of a few things that might help. I believe it's a two-step process: To begin, it's necessary to acknowledge that you're exhibiting an obsessive desire; subsequently, it's a matter of enhancing your harmonic passion.

There are obvious indicators that you're excessively committed to your profession. The following are some effective tests to help determine as much:

1. Do you have enough energy? Do you approach your task with a positive attitude? Do you take pleasure in your work?

2. Do you define yourself in ways other than via your work? If yourself is a pie, how much of it is taken up by your work?

3. Do you have healthy self-esteem? Obsessive passion is associated with a poor self-image, as well as automatic subconscious links between the self and the notion of "unpleasant."

4. Is your internal monologue optimistic when you work—loaded with phrases like "want to," "get to," and "can't wait to"? or are "must," "need," and "have to" strewn about?

5. Are you able to pause your job when you wish? Recent research discovered that while online gamers with a harmonious passion for gaming experienced positive emotions while playing, gamers with an obsessive passion experienced more negative emotions both while playing and when unable to play. Do you feel compelled to work constantly, even when you're not in the mood?

6. Do you find yourself in a state of flow? Do you feel as though time has passed you by, or do you feel the sensation of strain on your back? While flow is a pleasurable feeling, compulsive engagement feels more pressing.

If you're reading that list and thinking "no, no, no," these are indications that you may have an obsessive, rather than harmonious, interest. If you believe your level of obsessive passion is excessive, there are several things you can do:

- Include genuine breaks in your schedule. If you discover that you are obsessively committed to your work, force yourself out of that mindset by scheduling other activities throughout the day (like lunch with a friend or a break to hit the gym). Schedule time after work or on weekends for family, friends, and recreational activities. Maintaining a routine will help you stay accountable.

- Avoid bringing work home. If you can afford it, make it difficult for employees to access their work after they depart. Leave your laptop at home. Allow those files to remain on your desk. Stop browsing work email when at home (set up an out-of-office message on the off chance that you need to). Obsessive passion is a poor habit, and habits are easily broken.

- When you work, alter your mind patterns. Fake the harmoniously passionate person's thinking until you become one. Convert concepts of "must" and "need" to "want" and "want," for example. This may feel odd at first, but the overly enthusiastic thinking and the actions linked with it will soon fade away. According to a recent study, altering your explicit thought habits may boost self-esteem and harmonious passion.

- Take up a new pastime. Investing an excessive amount of self in a single undertaking frequently indicates a negative core self. The more activities outside of work that contribute to a positive sense of self, the less space your work performance takes up in your ego, and the less likely you'll be to experience burnout.

If you believe that all of this is incompatible with success, consider the following case study: A young, extremely talented musician, Yo-Yo Ma, is debating whether to pursue his promising solo career or defer it temporarily to gain a better understanding of the world around him. On the one hand, the music industry places a premium on time. Other talented artists could benefit from his decision to postpone his career. On the other hand, talent alone does not guarantee success in music. Audiences respond to skill and other subtle effects such as sensitivity, expression, and knowledge derived from non-musical experiences.

Finally, he elects to postpone his profession to broaden his sense of self. Ma compares those years to an "emotional bank account from which the rest of one's life must be withdrawn." To be honest, Ma's road wasn't entirely smooth; he scored a D+

in a Harvard music history course. However, I cannot discern whether those years of unrestrained study were detrimental to his career. Yo-Yo Ma is one of the world's best cellists, renowned not just for his extraordinary talent and dedication but also for the scope of his accomplishments, his compassion, wisdom, knowledge, and infectious optimism—in other words, his inseparable passions.

Passion is one of the primary vehicles to achieve excellence, creativity, imagination, and innovation. By no means am I advocating for a lack of passion. However, we rarely consider how other significant areas of life contribute to our primary passion. When a person's life is out of balance, passion can become obsessive and self-defeating. Passion is a wellspring of long-haul achievement when an individual can separate from their work and have a decent outlook on themselves.

Shh...

HOW TO GET RID OF AN OBSESSION

Being obsessive is similar to having tunnel vision: you lose the ability to notice or care about anything else. Obsession gets ingrained in your daily life and may be associated with dread; this is in contrast to addiction, which leads a person to feel unsatisfied until he indulges in the object of addiction. Overcoming an obsession isn't easy, but if you understand how to stop feeding the obsession and redirect your energy into new people and activities, liberation becomes a possibility.

Freeing Your Mind

It's key to distance yourself from the cause of your fixation. When you're obsessed with someone or something, being nearby can make thinking about anything else impossible. The closer you get to your fixation, the more difficult it will be to disengage from it. Distancing yourself physically from your passion will assist you in gaining mental distance as well. It will be difficult at first, but you will soon feel the obsession's influence begin to lessen gradually.

- Obsession with a certain individual is indicative of an unhealthy relationship. You should avoid interaction with someone who has acquired an unhealthy infatuation with you. Spend time diverting your attention to other activities, attempting to discover a method to progress to something else or something greater.

- Perhaps you're fascinated with a particular interest, such as playing a video game. If this is the case, remove the game from your sight by removing it from your computer or lending your console to a friend until your fixation subsides.

Put an end to its feeding. Because feeding an addiction provides a brief burst of pleasure, it's extremely difficult to break the habit. Simply contemplating the root of your fixation will bolster its hold on you. To end the infatuation, you must starve it. For instance, if you're enamored with a particular celebrity, refrain from discussing them with your pals. Put down your *Twitter* feed and quit fantasizing about what it would be like to date them. The more cognitive space you give your fixation, the more it will consume. Isolating your obsession's source of sustenance isn't an easy process. You may find yourself engaging in mental gymnastics, such as convincing yourself that you'll simply peek at someone's Facebook page one final time before putting an end to this fixation. However, if you want to overcome your passion, you must cut yourself off at the point of most indulgence. Occasionally, a fixation is so strong that it endures despite your best efforts to starve it. Regardless of how much you attempt to isolate yourself, your thoughts may return to your fixation. If this is the case, don't be too hard on yourself—you can still overcome your fixation; it will just take a little longer.

- Divert your attention away from your compulsive thoughts. Eliminating obsessive thinking is much easier said than done, however. When thinking and conversing about your favorite subject feels so fantastic, why would you ever want to stop? Keep in mind why you want to overcome the obsession: so you can look beyond it and enjoy the rest of your life. When the obsessive thoughts begin, prepare a few nice distractions so you don't tumble back down the rabbit hole. Here are some effective strategies to divert your attention:

- Engage in some form of physical activity that engages your brain as well. Running or walking may not be the greatest options, since you will have far too much time to reflect on your fixation. Consider rock climbing, caving, or participating in a team activity that requires both your mind and body to work together.

- Fictional works are superb diversionary devices. Pick up a new book or watch a video about a subject unrelated to your present obsession.

- When your thoughts begin to wander and you require an emergency distraction, consider blasting some music, calling a buddy (to discuss something other than your preoccupation), reading an entertaining news piece, or returning to work.

Concentrate on areas where you've been remiss. When you're consumed by an obsession, you have no time for anything else—like keeping up with work, establishing relationships, or exploring interests unrelated to the obsession. Once you begin devoting time to other aspects of your life, you'll find that you have less time to think about your fixation.

- Restoring neglected relationships is an excellent strategy to overcome an obsession. Your friends and family will welcome your return and will present you with fresh and exciting ideas, challenges, and drama to engage in. It'll be refreshing to consider something different for a change!

- Many people discover that burying themselves in work helps them avoid succumbing to obsessive thinking. Whatever work you're doing, put your all into it.

Acquire the ability to live in the moment. Are you prone to daydreaming? You can lose track of time thinking about someone or something you're enamored with for hours on end. However, when you sit in one spot and your thoughts are constantly elsewhere, you miss out on what is right in front of you. If you're ready to put an end to your obsession, cultivate the practice of mindfulness. It entails being present in the moment, rather than dwelling on the past or the future.

- Use all of your senses and truly feel what is happening around you. What are you currently smelling, seeing, hearing, and tasting? Rather than always thinking about something else, pay attention to what is happening directly in front of you.

- Pay close attention to what others are saying when they speak to you. Allow yourself to become interested in conversations rather than nodding absentmindedly with your head in the clouds.

- It may be beneficial to have a mantra that you can chant if your thoughts get obsessive. Repetition of a simple phrase such as "Breathe," "Connect to Now," or "I am here" may bring your attention back to the current moment.

Take advantage of cognitive behavior therapy (CBT). While this approach recognizes that there may be no way to quit thinking about addiction, it works to decrease the connection between obsessive thoughts and ordinary stressors. This makes it simpler to deal with daily life, think about and accomplish things; the preoccupation becomes more manageable.

CBT can also be used to construct a word or action that will "break" the obsessive thought and allow you to redirect your attention.

Developing New Habits

Consolidate your relationships with others. If you're fascinated with someone, spending time with another person is one of the most effective methods to change your mind. All of the energy you invested in your fixation will now be directed toward getting to know someone else. Enroll in a class, mingle at the dog park, or improve your relationship with existing buddies. Increasing your interaction with other people can let you appreciate how much more the world has to offer than your singular interest.

- Avoid making comparisons between new persons in your life and the person(s) with whom you're fascinated. Rather than attempting to mold them into another's shape, try to appreciate their unique features.

- Even if your passion is not a specific person, meeting new people can be beneficial. They'll present you with new perspectives and thoughts.

Pursue new passions. Perhaps "doing new things" appears to be a one-size-fits-all answer to every problem, but that's because it really can work. Learning a new skill or improving at a new pastime can stimulate your brain and cause a shift in perspective that can help you break out of your rut. Demonstrate to your fixation that it doesn't influence you by diverting your attention to other activities—anything that is unrelated to your passion.

- For instance, if you're obsessed with someone who despises visiting art museums and foreign films, this is your chance to engage in activities you've avoided in the past for that person's sake.
- If you're captivated by a particular subject, branch out and study something completely different.

Make modifications to your everyday routine. If your infatuation is driven in part by your habits, such as traveling the same route to work each day to pass through your ex's area, it's time to switch things up. Consider for a moment which behaviors need to be broken to avoid becoming hopelessly obsessed. You can certainly think of an answer immediately. Make a concerted attempt to alter your routine—it'll be difficult at first, but you should soon notice a difference in the intensity of your obsessive thoughts. Here are a few adjustments that may assist you in making a mental shift:

- Alternate your commute to work or school
- Exercise at a different gym or at a different time of day to avoid running into someone you're fascinated with.

- Every day, spend 15–20 minutes meditating with awareness.

- Rather than logging on first thing in the morning to check your email and immediately visiting your favorite websites, begin your day with meditation, a jog, or a walk with your dog.

- On weekends, visit a variety of different hangout areas.

- While working, listen to a variety of music. Redesign your life. If you're fed up with an obsession dictating your thoughts and behaviors, reclaim control via personal changes. While this may sound drastic, there are occasions when you need to alter your routine to demonstrate that you are still capable of doing so. Choose something in your life that is emblematic of your passion and do something to reintroduce it to the senses.

- Perhaps a makeover entails altering some aspect of your appearance for you. If you've been growing your hair long because you believe the person with whom you're infatuated prefers it that way, why not switch it up and cut it off? Develop a short, stylish style as you set out to acquaint yourself with the new you.

- If you spend your time online visiting the same websites repeatedly, it may be time to spruce up your room or office. Rearrange furniture and purchase a few new pieces. Clean and re-decorate your desk with new photographs or trinkets. Remove everything that serves as a reminder of what you'd rather not think about, and surround yourself with items that serve as a reminder that you're making progress.

Consult a therapist. Sometimes an obsession is so ingrained and tenacious that it is impossible to overcome on your own. If you're having difficulty controlling your obsession and it's interfering with your capacity to be joyful, make an appointment with a therapist. A skilled counselor can provide you with methods to reclaim control of your thoughts and reclaim control of your life.

Converting an Obsession into a Positive

Not all obsessions are negative; in fact, many people spend their life searching for their "passion"—that one thing that inspires them to continue learning and working. If you've discovered an obsession that gives you meaning, many would consider you extremely fortunate. For instance, if you live and breathe astronomy and would rather spend your time reading and learning about it than doing anything else, you may be able to turn your obsession into a lucrative business.

- Even if your obsession doesn't culminate in an astronomy Ph.D., you may still channel it into something beneficial. Perhaps you're infatuated with celebrity gossip and can't seem to put the tabloids down. Why not create a gossip blog or a *Twitter* account to share your findings?

- You might also use your obsession as a catalyst for self-improvement. If you're obsessed with someone who never looks your way, perhaps you'll decide to break some of your bad behaviors. Allow it to be your motivation to wake up early to go for morning runs before work or to read all the course material before class so you can speak intelligently.

Allow your obsession to serve as a creative muse. If your fixation with a particular individual, you could channel that energy into creating something lovely. Obsession lies at the heart of some of the greatest writing, art, and music in history. If you can't stop thinking about someone, channel your unrequited feelings into a poem, song, or painting.

Spend time with those who share your passion. A fixation may appear to be a problem until you discover a community of individuals who share your passion. Whatever you're fixated on, you're unlikely to be alone. Locate those who share your passions so you can share knowledge and constantly converse about them. Whether you're the biggest fan of a particular football club, can't stop watching everything a certain actress appears in, or stay up all night playing your favorite game, chances are that others share your enthusiasm.

Allow the fixation to not limit your world. A fixation becomes a problem only when it consumes all of your time and energy, leaving none for anything else. You are the only person who truly understands how much is excessive. If the subject of your fixation provides you delight and you still have time to meet your basic requirements and maintain friendships, it may be acceptable to simply let it run its course. However, if it leaves you feeling restricted, try to refrain from fueling the fires and allow yourself to enjoy something else for a bit.

Tips

- View it as a test and overcome it!
- Avoid fear and embarrassment.
- Don't ignore it; confront it.

- Expand your horizons: keep in mind that you had a fantastic life before the addiction.
- Act or think to dispel the thoughts.
- If necessary, proceed gently. You are not required to give up "cold turkey."
- Keep in mind that this is an ongoing process. Putting an end to a single-minded fixation does not happen immediately.
- Experiment with new activities to divert your attention from your addiction (e.g., socializing with friends, reading a book, or perhaps learning to play a musical instrument).

Warnings

- Obsessive-compulsive disorder and addiction are both serious problems that affect a large number of people. If you're unable to control your obsession(s) and/or they're causing you or those around you harm, seek professional treatment immediately.

Don't go yet; there's one thing left to do!

If you enjoyed this book or found it useful, I'd be very grateful if you'd post a short review on Amazon. Your support does make a difference, and I read all the reviews personally so I can get your feedback and make my titles even better.

Thanks again for your support!

If you enjoyed this title and would like to read about other topics that have changed my life, please check out my new books on *Amazon* or my website: www.my-mindguide.com.

Also, let's stay connected on social media. Please drop a line on *Facebook* or *Instagram*, and stay tuned for updates! You're welcome to share your thoughts with me directly as well: gassner@my-mindguide.com. In return, I'll send you a gorgeous infographic that you can frame.

Also, please leave a review on *Amazon*, as this will help me to reach an even broader audience. Thank you so much for your time, insight, and undying hunger for knowledge!

I want to say thank you to all of my colleagues, clients, friends, and family members, who have all contributed to what I am now.

I also want to say thank you to Gabriel Palacios, the king of hypnotherapy and a Swiss bestselling author who taught this old fox new tricks, letting me deep-dive into the mystery of hypnotherapy. I learned so much along the journey that I'm now a certified master-hypnosis coach and conversation coach myself!

Furthermore, I want to say thank you to the fantastic teachers of SAMYANA/Bali who trained me to become a certified yoga and meditation teacher.

Last but not least, I give a special thanks to my master-teacher Eckhard Wunderle, who's close to a saint to me. He introduced me to the world of meditation and let me discover all the wonders it has to offer. I couldn't be prouder about having received my certification as a meditation teacher from directly from him at the Institut für Spirituelle Psychologie.

Peace, love, and happiness to all of you—till next time!

AUTHORS PORTRAIT

Kurt Friedrich Gassner has worn many hats throughout his lifetime, including but not limited to serial entrepreneur, Creative Director, Meditation Teacher, Licensed Hypnotherapist, and more recently, self-improvement author. Leveraging his treasure trove of experiences and in-depth knowledge of psychology, he provides his readers with the tools they need to unlock their infinite potential.

As a prolific self-help writer, Kurt has authored the following books: *The Art of Forgiveness*, *Lie or Die*, *Soul-Match*, *Can You Inherit a Poisoned Mind?* and *The Power of Poverty*. He also authored a best-selling children's book in German-speaking countries and has over 20 books underway.

When it comes to enduring success, Kurt understands that financial prosperity isn't the only aspect one should strive for. He may be a self-made millionaire, but what really transformed his life is mastering his unconscious mind. Perseverance, personal power, self-awareness, and learning from past mistakes have all been key ingredients to bringing his dreams to fruition—and he strives to impart that wisdom onto others through his writing.

During his spare time, Kurt Friedrich Gassner is either traveling across the globe, golfing, biking in the Alps, hiking, or spending quality time with his loved ones. For the last 37 years, he has been happily married and he is the father of two successful children. Presently, he resides in both Munich, Germany, and Kirchberg, Austria.

OTHER BOOKS BY THE AUTHOR

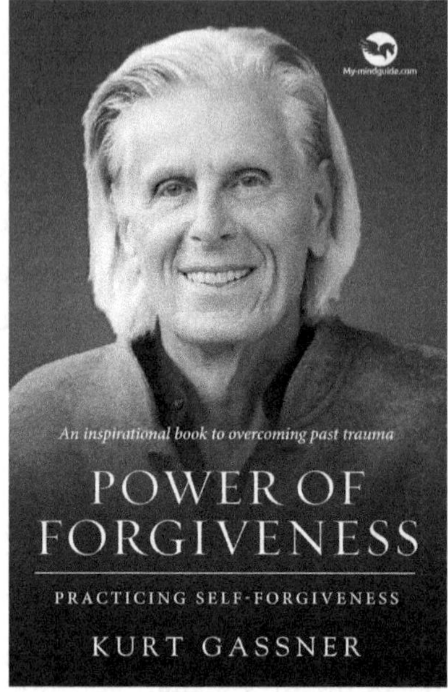

OTHER BOOKS BY THE AUTHOR

OTHER BOOKS BY THE AUTHOR

OTHER BOOKS BY THE AUTHOR

OTHER BOOKS BY THE AUTHOR

KURT GASSNER

Unlocking
The Healing
Power of Pets

What Pets Can Tell You About Your Soul

KURT GASSNER

Heilkraft
Unserer
Lieblinge

Was Haustiere über Ihre Seele verraten können

KURT GASSNER

OTHER BOOKS BY THE AUTHOR

BORN
in the
COLD
Liebe und Aufmerksamkeit in der Wachstumsphase eines Kindes
KURT GASSNER

BORN
in the
COLD
How to Tackle the Impact of the Absence of
Love and Attention in the Growing Stages of a Child's Life
KURT GASSNER

SOPHIAS WUNDERWELT
10 ERZÄHLUNGEN
KURT GASSNER

SOPHIA'S WONDERWORLD
10 TALES
KURT GASSNER

BESTSELLING AUTHOR OF
The Art Of
FORGIVNESS
AMAZON
#1
BESTSELLER
My-mindguide.com
A practical guide for
self healing and
overcome past traumas
The Art Of
FORGIVNES
KURT GASSNER
The Art Of
FORGIVNESS
KURT GASSNER

www.ingramcontent.com/pod-product-compliance
Lightning Source LLC
LaVergne TN
LVHW050549160826
845677LV00011B/2243

* 9 7 8 3 9 8 7 9 3 0 2 3 2 *